RETURN TO HELL

THE CHILLING SEQUEL TO
DEVIL'S DISCIPLES

Return to Hell

The continuing story
of Moors Murderers
Brady and Hindley

ROBERT WILSON

Javelin Books
LONDON · NEW YORK · SYDNEY

First published in the UK 1988 by Javelin Books, an imprint of Cassell plc,
Artillery House, Artillery Row, London SW1P 1RT

Distributed in the United States by
Sterling Publishing Co., Inc.,
2 Park Avenue, New York, NY 10016

Distributed in Australia by
Capricorn Link (Australia) Pty Ltd,
PO Box 665, Lane Cove, NSW 2066

British Library Cataloguing in Publication Data
Wilson, Robert, *1938–*
Devils disciples – part 2: return to hell.
1. Northern England. Murderers. Brady, Ian,
1938–, & Hindley, Myra, 1942–. Biographies
I. Title
364.1′523′0922

ISBN 0-7137-2073-5

Typeset by St. George Typesetting, Redruth, Cornwall

Printed in Great Britain by Cox & Wyman Ltd, Reading, Berks

CONTENTS

THE AUTHOR

ROBERT WILSON'S book *Devil's Disciples* shocked a whole new generation with the horror and tragedy of the Moors Murders, and reminded its parents and grandparents of the dreadful, almost unbelievable crimes that cost Ian Brady and Myra Hindley their freedom more than 22 years ago. Since his book was first published in April 1986, there have been further incredible developments. Once more the story has centred on Saddleworth Moor, a brooding, silent Pennine landscape where the victims of the ghastly lust of Brady and Hindley were buried. Now Robert Wilson, a journalist who first covered the sensational story when it broke in 1965, takes up again the harrowing, seemingly endless saga of the 'Devil's Disciples'.

ACKNOWLEDGEMENTS

GRATEFUL thanks to my colleagues and, yet again, the families of the young victims.

And in recognition of the eight-man team...
Detective Chief Inspector Geoffrey Knupfer
Detective Inspector Martin Flaherty
Detective Sergeant Gordon Mutch
Detective Sergeant Stephen Southward
Detective Sergeant Ronald Peel
Detective Constable Patrick Kelly
Detective Constable Gerard McGlynn
Detective Constable Alan Kibble.
And their leader, Detective Chief Superintendent Peter Topping, *who was right*.

I should like to thank the following for their kind permission to reproduce illustrations included in this book:-

the *Daily Star*, the *Daily Express*, the *Press Association*.

*We have made a covenant with death
and with hell are we at agreement.*

ISAIAH, 28:15.

THE HAUNTING

THE bony fingers paused, trembled and then picked up the envelope bearing the postmark of the city he had known so well, so long ago. He was curious, yet, he had said, afraid. He was fearful of the memories, of more nightmares, more voices in his head, and of the ghosts it would recall from his dreadful past.

The eyes, still cold and grey, but now set in gaunt sockets darkened by medication, took in the franking alongside the first-class stamp. *Manchester*. They flickered down to the name below. It had been a long time since anyone had addressed him as "mister".

Mr Ian Brady.

Those who guarded him had told him *who* had written the letter: a woman whose name he could never forget. A mother whose little daughter he had taken, degraded, tortured and finally killed.

They had also told him *why* she had written it, and it was this that haunted him. The eyes looked up from the letter that lay on the table of the hospital room in which, it seemed, he would end his days. The head turned slowly on the thin neck, to face to the east, while his mind travelled in distance to a place 40 miles away, in time to more than a quarter of a century ago.

Manchester, January, 1961. The place, the month, the year, would stay in his tormented memory for ever. It was there and then that he met *her*. *Myra Hindley*. He could still see that crown of bleached hair, lacquered and back-combed to frame the almost expressionless face, usually pale, but whipped pink by the wind on that icy winter's day. They had come face to face at Millward's Merchandise, in the little office where he worked as a stock clerk, where, on that fateful Monday morning, she had arrived as the new shorthand typist.

9

He was then 23, she 18. The thin lips tightened into a grimace. The memory of youth, however horribly mis-spent, was painful.

He had been cool towards her at first. There was no part for her in his life, no place for another to share his thoughts, his desires, his passions, his deeds. She didn't know a thing about him that day as she took off her coat, to reveal the wide-hipped figure that he was to come to know intimately. She didn't know that he'd been *deported*, just like the big shots in the gangster films and that he was biding his time and would one day show all those buggers, those cabbages, those morons. The Marquis de Sade, whose outlook he respected, had got it right: "*People are like maggots, small, blind, worthless fish bait.*"

Ian Brady's mind often returned to his beginnings, to Glasgow, the tough Gorbals where he'd been born on 2 January 1938, without a father to give him a name, and had grown up.

His mother, Margaret Stewart, was a tea room waitress who had been "taken advantage of" then left to bring up her baby alone, and to endure the shame, in pre-war Britain, of being an unmarried mother. As things turned out, she was to play little part in the rearing of her son. She had to carry on working to support them both so, at three months old, Ian was fostered out to her friend Mary Sloan and her family who lived in Camden Street in the grey granite tenements of the Gorbals.

When did it all start? When was he first consumed with this passion to hate, to hurt, to kill? The fair-haired lad, tall for his age, growing up in Glasgow during and after the war had been smugly satisfied by the shock and distaste of the other kids when he had sliced up caterpillars with razor blades, thrown cats from the third floor windows of the tenements or imprisoned them in mounds of stones in an old graveyard.

The authors and reporters always brought that up when they delved into his Scottish background. If only those sensation-seekers had known what he knew. He'd been good at keeping secrets. So very careful.

10

Brady looked down at the letter again, at the postmark. *Manchester*. He was almost 17 when he moved there – was 'deported' there – to live with his mother who had gone to that English city after marrying the man whose name he was to take, Patrick Brady. He had not had much choice, having been sent there by a court as a special condition to a probation order after the police had uncovered one of his secrets – his career as a housebreaker and petty thief.

The magistrates in Manchester, though, had not been so lenient and sent him to Borstal in 1956 for stealing from the vegetable market where his stepfather had helped him get a job. How sweet had been that freedom on his release two years later and how firm the resolve never to lose it again, to be so very much more careful, methodical.

From then on every crime would be perfect...In that instant of thought, Brady's mind snapped back to the present, to the letter still inside the envelope. *As perfect as*...NO. He must not think about that. Not now, not yet.

He remembered again that first meeting with Myra, who had been raised in the backstreets of Gorton, the grimy Manchester suburb where they worked together but, in those early days, seldom spoke. Not that he wanted her to. He had settled down well after Borstal and landed a job that paid twelve pounds a week. He had his own room at his mother's house in Westmoreland Street, Longsight and his records and his books: records of the German marching songs, of the speeches of Hitler, Goebbels and Himmler; books on cruelty, torture and death. His passion, his love affair with evil.

It had taken, he reflected, eleven months before he finally gave in to the coy glances, later the increased conversation and, finally, the approach from her: "Would you like to go out with me?"

He had been looking at her, too, those eleven months. Nice figure, despite the big arse. Not a bad face. The nose was a bit beaky, but he reckoned she was a virgin and that stirred him. OK. Why not? Best seats at the Essoldo. The film: *Judgement at Nurenberg*.

What a long time ago it had all been. And how readily, surprisingly, once he'd had her, he'd begun to share his secrets, his passion, with her. Even *his place*, a place he'd found on his motor-bike, a place 18 miles away, beyond the city, the towns, the villages, the farmhouses, up the twisting road, 1600 feet above sea level. A place that now sent a shiver through the frail body of Ian Brady at its recollection. A place that was to share their most awful secrets of all, whose name would one day always be linked with theirs. A place he thought he would never see again, but whose voices in the wind he still heard *Saddleworth Moor*.

Brady's hand shook as he took another of his favourite Gauloises from the packet, lit it from the still-smouldering butt of the last one. *Moors Murderer* Ian Brady, *Moors Murderess* Myra Hindley. Every story about them in every newspaper had always begun that way, for 21 years. Even the final ones, their obituaries, would begin that way.

Back in the summer of 1963, though, they were just Ian and Myra – Myra, whose name hadn't even been in the *Gorton and Openshaw Reporter*. A nice young couple, the Lancashire lassie and her Scots laddie, most people thought, including a young girl who lived a few streets away from Myra. *Pauline R...*

NO, NO, NO. A shutter slammed down frighteningly in Ian Brady's mind. He must not think about her. Not now. He *would not* think about her.

That long-ago summer Ian Brady had taken his suitcase, his camera, his tape recorder, across the city from Longsight and moved in with Myra and her grandmother – though frail, old Mrs Ellen Maybury never realised it – at Number 7, Bannock Street, Gorton.

But Maureen, Myra's younger sister, knew they were living together. Maureen, pretty, prettier than Myra, had married *him*, *David Smith*. In those days Smith had lived next-door-but-one to *Pauline R...*

NO!

The name haunted him, tore at what remained of his soul. He must shut it from his mind. Like the date, *12 July*

1963, and a headline he had sought palpitatingly, that appeared in the *Manchester Evening News* a few nights later: *Girl, 16, vanishes on way to jive club.*

Brady glanced down at the letter again, then, very slowly, back to the east. His mind's eye now beyond Gorton, beyond Manchester, the towns, the villages, the farmhouses, upwards, to the place that still shared his, no *their*, secret. A place where they had met the Devil. *Saddleworth Moor.*

Chapter One

PAULINE

12 July 1963

THE drizzle had long since dried from the uneven flagged pavements and a watery sun had dipped slowly behind the tall buildings of the city centre in the distance, the sun's dimming light casting pastel shadows. Its occasional appearances between showers that summer's day had brightened even the sooty Victorian drabness of the rows and rows of terraced slums, criss-crossed by the maze of cobbled streets that made up the sprawling, untidy patchwork of the Manchester suburb of Gorton.

The lights had gone on in the Steel Works Tavern, filled with customers now that the men had watched *Bonanza* and their wives and girlfriends had dabbed their eyes at *Emergency Ward 10*. The clink of glasses and the shouts of laughter from men and women who, in those days, had jobs and were glad that it was Friday and they had a lie-in in the morning, drifted across Wiles Street.

The night air was still warm and the voice from a black and white television set proclaiming that "Nothing Acts Faster than Anadin" drifted from an open sash window. Quite a few of the residents of Gorton would need Anadin the next morning!

It was still light and the late evening held a faint promise of sunshine next day. In the distance a dog barked and a cat that had just padded from one of the backyards stretched, then fled in mid-yawn as the cheerfully whistling bespectacled teenager approached, his pursed lips giving way to a smile as he recalled the comic antics he had just seen at the pictures.

The sounds of revelry from the pub were drowned as, at the end of the street, a train rattled noisily by on the Belle Vue to Piccadilly line at the foot of the embankment, guarded for safety by a fence of upright railway sleepers that did little to deter the nimble, wiry back-street kids.

Paul Reade was feeling pleased with himself. He was 15 and had just drawn his first week's wages. Two pounds and seventeen shillings. And it had, as his dad would say, burnt a hole in his pocket. In those days of fuller employment, it was the custom in many homes for a lad who had just started to work to keep his first pay packet. His mam and dad, Joan and Amos Reade, had taken little persuading to abide by the tradition.

The lad had, in fact, worked for two weeks at the local upholstery works, but had had to keep 'a week in hand' before the brown envelope with two pound notes, one ten-shilling note, two half-crowns and a two-shilling piece had been handed to him by his satisfied employer. And that night Paul had spent quite a bit of it.

He had decided to treat his mates, brothers David and Graham Cummings. His elder sister Pauline had been getting ready to go to a dance, a jive they called it, at the local Railway Institute as the new wage earner had left the two-up, two-down house, Number 9, Wiles Street, earlier that night.

There was a strict house rule. Paul had to be in by ten, his sister by eleven. There was no need for a reminder as he set off to join his pals.

Amos Reade was a baker at Sharples and had to be up at three in the morning to help bake the bread for the city's shops. He liked to sleep knowing that both his son and his daughter were back safely under his roof.

Pauline was growing up now, thought Joan as she watched the slim, blue-eyed girl get ready for the dance, brushing her soft brown hair until it shone like the mahogany upright piano that took pride of place – next to the Catholic pictures facing it – in the little square parlour.

She was doing well, was our Pauline, reflected Joan. They were pleased with her at the bakery where she had joined her dad as a trainee. She was a good worker, a pleasant girl, good to her mam and dad. And, she told herself with pride, a bonnie lass, too.

Pauline loved her family. She would get up in the mornings, make a pot of tea in the back kitchen and have a half-hour chat with her ailing mother before setting off for work. She was a quiet girl, but not one to be picked on at Peacock Street Primary School, St. James's Secondary Modern and later St. Francis's. Now she was working, her confidence and sense of independence were growing. "Our kid can stick up for herself," her brother Paul would say.

That night, she was wearing a pink dress, threaded with gold lurex, with a square neckline – distinctive from the twenty-nine-and-eleven frocks a lot of girls wore – beneath a lavender woollen cardigan. As was the fashion, she wore a pair of long dress gloves, white to match her high-heeled shoes, and a gold-coloured belt-chain, necklace and ring.

"You look nice love," said Joan approvingly. Pauline gave a slight shrug of teenage indifference, for she was disappointed. Her friend, Pat Cummings, whose brothers had gone to the pictures with Paul, had just told her that she couldn't go to the dance.

Pauline's mother had a suggestion. Why not see if Linda Leadbetter or Linda Bradshaw could go? They only lived in nearby Taylor Street.

The *Dickie Henderson Show* was just about to start on Channel Nine as Pauline slipped on her powder-blue coat and white chiffon headscarf. "Shan't be long," Joan called to Amos, who was about to go to bed, then mother and daughter walked together to Taylor Street. More disappointment for the teenager. Her two other friends couldn't go either.

Pauline looked at her mother and, uncharacteristically, announced: "I'll go on my own, mam." Joan Reade hesitated, but then reasoned to herself that her daughter was bound to meet someone she knew. There were the usual mother's cautionary words: "Mind what you're doing. Be home for eleven."

And so, with ten shillings in her purse for lemonade and crisps, Pauline Reade left her mam.

Her route to the Railway Institute, the local

railwaymen's social club, less than half a mile from her home, took her into Gorton Lane and past Bannock Street on the right. It was being said that her friend Maureen's elder sister had started living with a Scottish bloke at Number 7. On past the foundry, then left at Froxmer Street with the Vulcan pub on the corner, Pauline Catherine Reade vanished from her mother's sight.

PAUL and his pals had gone to see Harold Lloyd's *World of Comedy* and *The Westerners* at the Essoldo. The main feature had already started when they took their seats in the one-and-sixes, so they watched the continuous performance up to the point where they had gone in. Paul nudged his companions and nodded towards the exit.

Outside, they blinked at each other in the watery, fading sunlight. There was time for a fish and chip supper. The treat was on Paul, checking his pocket to make sure the remainder of his wages was still there.

The city lads threaded their way through the streets of Gorton to the chippy with its white-scrubbed tables, where customers could sit down instead of eating their fish and chips from the paper outside.

They talked, as young lads do, about the film they had just seen, about what they were doing tomorrow and Sunday, and about girls, Paul idly wondering to himself whether his sister was having a good time at the dance.

He looked up at the clock on the chip shop wall. Time to go. And so, at 9.30, Paul Reade, a contented, happy lad with a job, a good mam and dad and a smashing sister, said goodnight to his pals in Taylor Street and strode, a spring in his step, past the noisy, cheerful hullabaloo of the Steel Works Tavern.

"By bloody 'ell," somebody was saying inside. "What about that Christine Keeler and that Mandy Rice-Davies? That Profumo bloke's made a right bugger o' things."

"Still," another Chesters bitter-soaked Mancunian male

voice joined in, "that Christine Keeler's a bit of all right. A bloody fit piece..."

A female voice interrupted. "It's the wives *I* feel sorry for," sympathising with film star Valerie Hobson, whose husband, War Minister John Profumo's career was on the line because of his involvement with the good-time girls.

Paul turned into Charmers Street, round the corner from Wiles Street. It was a quarter to ten. There was a young woman standing there, her face expressionless, her eyes cold without greeting as, in the twilight, they met those of the teenager. Paul knew her, though not all that well nowadays. She was six years his senior, but they had played together with the other kids when they were younger. He remembered her as bossy, always wanting to be leader of the pack. Now she was grown up, 'sophisticated', snotty, and living with her gran at 7 Bannock Street and, though the old woman didn't know it, that Scottish bloke was sleeping there.

She was breaking the law too, not that many people realised it, for though she hadn't passed her test, she was driving about in that old Ford van one of the neighbours had lent her, without L plates. However, as things turned out, it was a trivial offence compared to how she had used and where she had been with that five-hundredweight van that night. Something that the blissfully ignorant Paul Reade knew nothing about, then.

No word passed between them as he walked past the girl, eleven days from her twenty-first birthday, standing almost like a sentry and looking down Wiles Street.

Bloody stuck up Myra Hindley.

THE teenager took his usual route, cutting through Timothy Street then intending to go through the entry at the back of the end house, Number 13, two doors from where he lived. But his stride shortened and slowed as he approached the entry. He could hear raised voices. Perhaps the lad from Number 13 would be canoodling, or arguing, with his girlfriend. The other lads were scared of *him* and Paul Reade was no exception.

His name was David Smith, and though only six days older than Paul, he was tougher, stronger, street-wise and had a streak of violence. He lived there with his father, Jack, and his girlfriend was Maureen Hindley, Myra's 17-year-old sister. They had grown up together, played together in the dingy Gorton back-streets – Paul, Pauline, Maureen, David and the other kids. But now the wiry, dark-haired Smith seemed so much older than Paul.

The lad did not want to risk upsetting him so he turned on his heel and retraced his steps to enter Wiles Street from the opposite end. Past Blower's corner shop, closed for the night, and the terraced houses, some now with drawn curtains, to Number 9. As he had promised his mam and dad, Paul Reade was home, and safe, by ten o'clock.

The neighbours who were not in the pubs – or at the Railway Institute dance – settled down to watch Vince Hill and Tommy Bruce in *Stars and Garters*, but Paul, tired from his week's graft at the upholstery works, went to bed.

It was around midnight when the dozing youngster was gently awakened by his mother. He yawned, looked at the clock. "What's up, mam?" Joan Reade, who had not been well lately, was worried. "Our Pauline's not home. It's not like her. She said she'd be in by eleven."

Surely she'd be all right, reasoned Paul. She was with friends. Wasn't she? His mother shook her head. Pauline had gone on her own.

Paul was to recall to me later: "It was so unlike our kid to go on her own like that. It was just not in her nature. Nor was it like her to be late. My mam and I got dressed and went out to look for her. We didn't want to wake my dad because he had to be up so early."

Mother and son half walked, half ran, through the now dark streets, past the closed and silent Steel Works Tavern, along Gorton Lane, Froxmer Street, Railway Street and into Cornwall Street where the social club stood and where the dance was over. They could see a light inside and a figure, that of the steward cleaning up. Joan and Paul hammered on the door, the sound echoing through the empty building. They stood in the darkness, waiting, wondering, until the lock clicked back and the door opened.

Mrs Reade knew the man. "Do you know if Pauline Reade has been in here tonight?' The man shook his head. No, he hadn't seen her.

Paul and his mother looked at each other. Her unease had now been replaced by a slow, nauseating, stomach-tightening fear. Where *was* Pauline? For God's sake. *Where was she*?

For two-and-a-half hours, Joan, Paul and now Amos Reade went from street to street, door to door, friend to friend. And, frantic with worry, at 2.30am, Joan went to the phone box and called the police.

Friday, 12 July 1963, was just one more day in a year with so much news, so much to talk about. The year of the Profumo scandal, the year the beloved Pope John died, the year the first woman went into space, the year when President John F. Kennedy was cut down by an assassin's bullet in Dallas, Texas, the year when four mop-haired lads from Liverpool who called themselves the Beatles revolutionised popular music. But that Saturday night in the Steel Works Tavern they would be talking, this time in quieter tones, about something that had happened much, much, closer to home, though little realising its full, horrifying eventual significance.

For Friday, 12 July 1963 was the last time anyone ever saw Pauline Reade alive. And most of the young couples in the Steel Works Tavern would be grandparents before her terrible fate was finally discovered.

THE police were reassuring, friendly, when they arrived at 9 Wiles Street. Well, they said, Pauline *was* 16. Boyfriends? Joan Reade shook her head. Was she in any trouble? Not that anyone knew of, said her parents.

Pauline was a good girl. She kept no secrets and confided in her mam.

The search was comparatively low-key. Missing teenage girls were not uncommon. They usually turned up somewhere, broke, disillusioned, tearful. But usually alive. A file was opened on Pauline Reade, missing person. *Christ*, they were to say later, if only they'd known what had gone on that night in those Gorton backstreets.

The police did, though, make intensive inquiries. They dragged the canal in Cornwall Street, talked to all Pauline's friends, had posters printed. But the disappearance of Pauline Reade made only a few inches on the bottom half of page one of the *Manchester Evening News* the following Wednesday, 17 July, under the double-column headline: "Girl, 16, Vanishes on Way to Jive Club."

Joan Reade, though, with a mother's intuition, *knew* that this was not just another case of a missing teenage girl seeking adventure, kicking over the traces, looking for excitement, new experiences somewhere else. Pauline had loved her home, her family. She hadn't run away, and if she had, she must have had a very good reason.

But in the months, that became years, to follow she liked to think that that was really the case: that Pauline had run away. It was a mother, thinking, even wishing, the worst of her daughter just so, *please, God*, she could somehow, somewhere still be alive, and would one day, as if nothing had happened, walk through the front door of Number 9 and say "Hello mam, dad", in her pink dance dress.

Joan's fervent prayer that this was the simple truth of the matter, the mystery, became an obsession. Every hour of every day she looked and looked and looked, peering into the faces of everyone she passed, staring through every shop window to try to catch a glimpse, a clue, that would lead her to her missing daughter.

Sometimes she would think she had caught sight of Pauline through the steamy window of a red Manchester corporation bus, and would chase after it down Ashton Old Road shouting: "Pauline, Pauline, PAULINE..."

Every rumour, every reported sighting was pursued by the distraught mother. If someone said they had seen a girl who looked like Pauline in Ancoats, Bradford, Longsight, Openshaw or any other of the city suburbs, she would get on the bus and go there, scanning every fellow-passenger, gazing long and hard into every female face.

Never, though, in her most fearsome nightmares, of which there were many, could she *ever* have dreamt what had happened to Pauline, so close to home.

And when she did it was just too much to bear.

THE letter in front of Ian Brady was still unread, his sick mind still lingering in that summer of 1963 and beyond, when he and Myra shared so many secrets, when she was his completely. What was it she had said later? "*I had no sexual experience. I was still a virgin. I fell hopelessly in love with Ian Brady, practically from setting my eyes on him...he became my god, my idol, my object of worship. He could have told me that the earth was flat, that the moon was made of green cheese, that the sun rose in the west and I would have believed him. Such were the powers of his persuasion.*"

She used to call him Neddy after the character on his favourite radio programme, *The Goon Show*, and he had called her Hess, the name of Hitler's deputy. (It was doubtful, though, that the frail old man whose life in solitary incarceration ended recently, could have taught Myra Hindley much about evil.)

In 1963, Neddy and Hess were inseparable and went everywhere together, mainly to the Pennine Moors that flanked Manchester, to Derbyshire and Yorkshire, and especially to Saddleworth. She'd soon acquired a taste for the German wine they drank together on their moorland picnics, and for his other insatiable appetites, like pornographic photographs. He'd taken photographs of her in her gran's parlour while the old woman was asleep upstairs; she'd taken them of him and he'd taken pictures of them together, using the timer on his camera. But these sordid pleasures were innocent pastimes compared with the other passion he was sharing with her.

Pauline Reade. His mind shrank from the name, the memory of that warm July night when he and Myra shared a secret so loathsome, so vile that there could be no forgiveness by anyone, mortal or immortal; for a deed of the Devil that began among the smoke-blackened terraces of Gorton and ended on Saddleworth Moor.

There could be no forgiveness from the mothers, like the one who had written to him, the mother of *another* girl who must hate him with all her heart for what he had done to her little girl. And like the mother of the boy. *John Kilbride*. Again the voices came, from two decades ago. "*I am a police officer. We are making inquiries about the disappearance of a young boy...*"

That had been on 23 November 1963, four months and eleven days after Pauline. The difference was that the police *knew* about John Kilbride. They had *found* him.

It was on a Saturday afternoon sixteen days after Myra passed her driving test – he never had learned to drive – that they hired a Ford Anglia and drove to the market at Ashton-under-Lyne, a town close to Gorton, and on the way to Saddleworth. The lad had been twelve and so friendly, so trusting.

On that dark, chill winter night there had been a passenger in the Anglia as it wound its way up the steep, twisting moorland road to Saddleworth Moor. A boy who was to endure the warped sexual pleasure of Ian Brady and, finally, to satisfy his fiendish lust to kill. The monster dug another grave.

Brady's eyes returned to the table, the letter, and he thought of another letter he had received, from another mother. He had been unable to read that either, he said. It, too, jarred a memory he tried desperately to blot from his confused mind, his conscience. *That* had been a month after he and Myra had got new transport, better than that old Ford van she had finally bought, but kept for only a few months, better than hiring a car, better than the Austin

23

A40 they got in February. The new vehicle had been a white Morris Mini-van. The perfect transport.

Keith B...... The shutter came down on his brain again.

NO!

Chapter Two

KEITH

16 June 1964

WEARILY Winifred Johnson shrugged into her coat and glanced round at her first-born. "Come on, Keith," she told her young son, looking so different, more impish, without his wire-rimmed National Health spectacles. "We'd better be going. Your gran'll wonder where you are."

Winnie was pregnant again. At 30, she was expecting her seventh child, due in two weeks. She was tired and her back ached, but she was determined that her short-sighted son should not step into danger. To get to his gran's Keith had to cross Stockport Road, buzzing day and night with an endless stream of traffic, and he had broken his glasses a few days earlier at the swimming baths.

Keith Bennett was 12 years old and lived with his mother, his stepfather, out-of-work joiner Jim Johnson and his brothers and sisters at Number 29 Eston Street in the Chorlton-on-Medlock district of Manchester. It was the end house of the terrace, a cul-de-sac which ended just beyond their front door with a high brick wall that had worn out more of her children's shoe toes than Winnie cared to remember.

Keith was going to spend the night with his grandmother, Mrs Gertrude Bennett, who lived a quarter of a mile away in Morton Street, Longsight. He was devoted to his gran and enjoyed staying with her and it was a common arrangement for poorer families with little room in their small, rented homes. He was a quiet, thoughtful lad who helped his mother with jobs around the house and was not one to 'run wild' with the tougher kids in the neighbourhood. He usually played close to his home with the neighbours' children and preferred quieter pursuits, like gardening and drawing, to boisterous, rowdy games.

It was a mild summer night, just as it had been eleven months earlier when Pauline Reade left her home less than a mile-and-a-half away, when mother and son stepped out of the front door of 29 Eston Street, he for the last time.

A boy from Ashton-under-Lyne, John Kilbride, the same age as Keith, had gone missing the previous November. It had been in all the newspapers and there had been posters everywhere: "*Have you seen this boy?*" Winnie, like thousands of other mothers, had seen the photographs of Sheila Kilbride, the sadness, the pain in her eyes. Poor woman. How must she feel? Then there was that girl from Gorton, Pauline Reade. Her mother must be going through agony, too.

But Winnie, sandy-haired and homely, had a bigger fear for her children just then – a dread of them being knocked down on Stockport Road, the bustling artery linking the 'posher' environs of Cheshire with central Manchester. She worried particularly about Keith because of his poor eyesight. He must get some new glasses as quickly as possible.

The pair turned out of Eston Street into Hathersage Road, across Plymouth Grove, along Plymouth Grove West, then stood on the pavement waiting for the flow of traffic to ease. "Now think on," Winnie told her son, "be careful. Watch the traffic."

Keith Bennett squinted at his mother. "See you tomorrow, mam." Winnie gave the little lad a hug and a kiss. A car stopped at the pedestrian crossing, a van came to a halt from the other direction. "Right, off you go." She watched him safely reach the opposite pavement. He was out of danger now, she thought, as she saw Keith, in his blue jeans, T-shirt and new white jerkin, turn into the opening on the other side of the road, one of two short side-streets leading to Morton Street where his gran lived. He had less than 200 yards to walk.

But his route was to take him along a thoroughfare far

more dangerous, lethal, than the menace of the cars, vans, lorries and buses of Stockport Road. The narrow street of bay-windowed houses into which he had turned was Westmoreland Street.

It was there, that until about a year ago, Ian Brady had lived at Number 18. He still called to see his mother and stepfather. Myra Hindley drove him there, though she always remained outside in her white Mini-van.

And, at around a quarter to eight on Tuesday, 16 June 1964, four days after his twelfth birthday and with just a shilling in his pocket, Keith Bennett vanished from the face of the earth, "as if," the bewildered police were to say later, "a flying saucer came down and spirited him away."

But Keith Bennett had been spirited away in a far more earthly form of transport.

A white Mini-van.

MRS Gertrude Bennett glanced at the clock on the mantelpiece. Eight thirty and still no sign of her young grandson. He mustn't be coming after all. She was not unduly worried, just disappointed that she wouldn't see him that night.

She and her daughter, a quarter of a mile apart, went to their beds with untroubled minds, neither of them dreaming that, in those 200 yards that had separated them, young Keith had fallen into the clutches of a terrible evil.

Next morning, Winnie went to her mother's home to collect Keith. She was met by a puzzled stare. Keith? No, Mrs Gertrude Bennett hadn't seen him. She just thought he'd changed his mind, that they'd made other arrangements...

Winnie hurried, as fast as her condition would allow, to Victoria Park Secondary Modern School. No, he had not turned up there, either. Panic gripped her. She knew that Keith had not gone off on some mischievous escapade. He was just not that sort.

There and then she knew, as she has always known, that something dreadful had happened to her son.

The police launched a huge search, conducted house-to-house inquiries, combed buildings in the area, dragged reservoirs and canals, put up posters and distributed thousands of leaflets bearing Keith's photograph with the question: "Have you seen this boy?" The face of Keith Bennett, in his wire-rimmed glasses, became as familiar a sight in Manchester then as the advertisements on the hoardings for Watney's Red Barrel or Nelson cigarettes.

Then the police began to wonder: could there be a link between Keith's disappearance and that of John Kilbride whose case had baffled Lancashire detectives for seven months? He had lived only eight miles from the Manchester boy. They were both the same age, both had vanished in the evening, both were happy at home and neither had ever even threatened to run away.

Winnie Johnson went to see Sheila Kilbride, the quietly-spoken mother of John, the eldest of her seven children. She had not seen him since the Saturday afternoon in November when he set off to go to a cinema matinee in Ashton town centre with his pal John Ryan. The two women each knew how the other felt, of the heartbreak, the uncertainty. They had much in common, but far, far more than either of them realised.

The police brought out all the files of missing youngsters. *Pauline Read, John Kilbride, Keith Bennett*. Was there a link?

The search for Keith went on, in a year when Prince Edward was born, Ian Smith became Prime Minister of Rhodesia, BBC2 first went on the air, Nelson Mandela began life imprisonment and Harold Wilson moved into 10 Downing Street. Such a long, long time ago.

"We are investigating every possible explanation," said the police, adding with tragic understatement: "Crime cannot be ruled out..." And: "We are determined to find this boy quickly."

It is a sad fact that, more than twenty-four years later, it is now *known* that crime of the most dreadful kind *was* committed. And that the police, who had been determined to find him quickly, are still looking for Keith Bennett.

★　　★　　★

AROUND the sad Johnson family the face of Manchester was changing. The slums were being demolished and families were being moved out of the city to new townships, overspill estates specially built to replace the rows of terraces that were being bulldozed. The newest settlement was Hattersley, on the outskirts of the Cheshire town of Hyde, ten miles from Manchester. The wagon trains of furniture removal vans were moving east – and in one of them the belongings of granny Ellen Maybury, her grandaughter Myra Hindley and the girl's surly Scottish boyfriend, Ian Brady. They moved, in September, 1964, to the end house of a terrace of four, 16 Wardle Brook Avenue. An address that one day would be more infamous than 10 Rillington Place, the home of mass murderer John Reginald Halliday Christie.

Winnie Johnson, though, by now a mother for the seventh time, did not want to move. Like Joan Reade she clung to the hope that one day her short-sighted son would be standing on the doorstep of 29 Eston Street...

Keith was everywhere, but nowhere. His photograph smiled at her from posters, it seemed, on every street. She saw his face in her dreams, heard his voice, calling "Mam", then awoke from the dreams to the nightmare of her waking hours. "If only I'd known, I'd never have let him out of my sight," she would sigh.

Somehow, she got through Christmas Eve, Christmas Day, Boxing Day, trying her best to bring festive cheer to her other children, but finding it impossible to blot out her mind's eye picture of how happy Keith would have been with his presents, his family.

And then, the day after Boxing Day, another newspaper headline. Another missing child in Manchester.

The child, a girl, read Winnie, had disappeared from a travelling fair near her home in Ancoats, on the other side of the city. And her disappearance was every bit as baffling as that of Keith's.

The little girl was ten and her name was Lesley Ann Downey. Now four mothers, within a few miles of each other, had spent the most miserable, heartbreaking Christmas of their lives.

Again it was the familiar pattern. Frogmen in the canal, posters printed, house-to-house inquiries, stories in the newspapers, pictures of a sad-eyed, bewildered mother.

Winnie Johnson knew exactly how she felt.

THE three files on the desk of the man in charge of Manchester CID had become well-thumbed. Detective Chief Superintendent Douglas Nimmo could not forget them, found it hard to lay them down. Three names: *Pauline Reade, Keith Bennett, Lesley Ann Downey.* Three children missing on his patch and not the faintest whisper of a clue as to where any of them could be. He had talked and talked to the mothers, read and re-read the statements, gone back over and over the same ground. Nothing.

"Doug" Nimmo, a tall, softly-spoken Scotsman, took over as CID chief in 1965 with a hard-won reputation for never letting go once he had started an investigation. The son of an Edinburgh bank manager, he had chosen the police force as a career 29 years earlier. He was also a deeply caring man who shared the grief of families whose lives had been shattered by crime while trying – and very often succeeding – to bring the culprits to justice.

He was 54, had been married for 27 years, with a son and daughter. His wife, Ella, was resigned to sharing him with his other love, his job. It was very often murder that got in the way of a planned night out with friends and was responsible for countless spoiled dinners.

With the daily crime and the growing vice of one of Britain's biggest cities to contend with, Nimmo spared whatever time he could to the three baffling cases. And to offering words of comfort to the three mothers, now numb with grief and the heartbreaking frustration of not knowing what had happened to their children. If only there was a clue, a slender lead that might just point him and his detectives in the right direction.

The routine continued. Burglaries, robberies, assaults, attacks, shootings, stabbings, frauds and an ever-watchful eye on the night club scene for which Manchester, in the 'swinging sixties' was noted as being the high spot outside the capital.

But never far from the mind of Nimmo were the tragic, sad faces of those three mothers he wanted so much to help. Somebody, somewhere *must* know something...

And then, in the autumn of 1965, the lead he had been seeking came. And it pointed in a direction, to a place, a series of events, a possibility, then a probability when the full facts emerged, that made the blood of Nimmo, who thought he had seen and heard everything in nearly 30 years as a copper, turn to ice.

Ten miles away, at Hattersley, a few miles outside his patch, Cheshire police had arrested a man and charged him with murder. And the lad who had shopped him had been telling an amazing story, so incredible, they were finding it hard to believe. But, as they were to discover, every word of the most evil tale of crime they had ever heard was true. The activities of a man called Ian Brady and a woman called Myra Hindley were over. For the police they were only just beginning

Their investigations, following that arrest, on 7 October 1965, were to unfold a calendar of horror that shocked the whole world.

23 November 1963: John Kilbride, twelve, was picked up on the market ground at Ashton-under-Lyne, murdered by Ian Brady and buried on Saddleworth Moor.

26 December 1964: Lesley Ann Downey, ten, was lured away from a fairground in Ancoats, Manchester by Ian Brady and Myra Hindley. She was taken to their council house home, 16 Wardle Brook Avenue, Hattersley, where she was stripped, photographed, her last moments tape-recorded.

31

Then they killed her and buried her on Saddleworth Moor.

6 October 1965: Edward Evans, seventeen, was picked up at Central Station, Manchester, driven to 16 Wardle Brook Avenue and murdered by Ian Brady and Myra Hindley.

7 October 1965: David Smith, the seventeen-year-old brother-in-law of Myra Hindley made a frantic dawn telephone call to the police. He had witnessed the murder of Evans, and Brady had boasted to him of "killing people and burying their bodies on the moors."

The police found the body of Evans, trussed up and wrapped in a blanket, in a bedroom of 16 Wardle Brook Avenue. He had fourteen horrendous axe wounds to the head. Then they found an exercise book containing drawings, doodles, names idly scrawled by Ian Brady, most of them the names of film stars. Except one. *John Kilbride*.

The detectives also found a tartan-backed photograph album with pictures of Brady and Hindley, some of them on the moors... A search began in the Pennines.

15 October 1965: The search was switched to Saddleworth Moor after 12-year-old Patricia Hodges, who had lived two doors from Brady and Hindley at Hattersley, took the police to the spot where the couple had taken her for picnics.

16 October 1965: The body of Lesley Ann Downey was found in a shallow grave at Hollin Brow Knoll, close to the spot where Patricia had picnicked with the killers. Meanwhile at 16 Wardle Brook Avenue, a detective found, tucked between the cover and the spine of Myra Hindley's prayer book, a railway station left-luggage ticket. It led them to two suitcases at Manchester's Central station which contained the murderers' souvenirs of evil – including photographs of the naked body of Lesley Ann Downey and the tape recording of her last words.

21 October 1965: The body of John Kilbride was found, 373 yards away and on the opposite side of the moorland road from the grave of Lesley Ann. The burial spot was pinpointed through a photograph of Myra Hindley

holding a puppy, taken from the tartan-backed album. She had been pictured, by Ian Brady, squatting and staring at the ground at the exact spot where John Kilbride was buried.

It was all damning evidence to which there could be only one outcome for the couple in custody. But for Douglas Nimmo, that calendar of evil was incomplete. Two dates, two names, were missing from the amazing dossier of fact:

12 July 1963: Pauline Reade
16 June 1964: Keith Bennett.

THE search of Saddleworth Moor went on, commanded by Detective Chief Superintendent Arthur Benfield, head of Cheshire CID. The police officers *knew* that Pauline Reade had been murdered four months before John Kilbride and that Keith Bennett had met his death seven months after John and six months before Lesley Ann Downey. They also knew that their bodies, too, had been buried.

There was no doubt in the mind of Nimmo, or in that of any other policeman, that on their last short walks Pauline and Keith had shared the same fate as the three other victims. And even though winter was closing in, he was not prepared to let go, yet. More than 100 policemen in the biggest combined police operation ever mounted in a search still combed the moorland. Teams were also hunting in the area of the Snake Pass in Derbyshire and Woodhead, Cheshire, identified on other photographs taken by Brady.

Overhead, Canberra and Victor planes of the Royal Air Force droned, their crews taking hundreds of aerial pictures to try to detect alterations in the Pennine landscape that might indicate the locations of more graves. Hikers, ramblers and members of mountain rescue teams joined in the search, and the policemen were now using special probing rods made by local mill engineer Victor Hird. The rods had bulbous ends to which tell-tale particles of earth would stick and had been developed with the cooperation of the War Graves Commission which, 20 years earlier, had had a similar grisly task in Europe. Saddleworth Moor had become honeycombed with the marks of the excavation, but if that dark, sullen Pennine landscape was holding more grim secrets it was refusing to reveal them. And so were Ian Brady and Myra Hindley.

The calm, pipe-smoking Nimmo had spent weeks on the Moor, 20 miles from his office. They had dug up the neatly-laid gardens of 16 Wardle Brook Avenue, Hattersley.

Beneath Nimmo's outward calm was a nagging frustration. He and his detectives had been through 13 Wiles Street, Gorton, now empty, with a fine-tooth comb. And – blast it – Bannock Street, where Number 7 could have held such vital clues, was now a wasteland of rubble as Gorton's slums fell beneath the bulldozers.

Police had then reopened the files on a number of missing people, looking for a 'common factor.' The common factor linking Pauline and Keith with the known victims shouted out at them. As Nimmo was to say much later: "I am certain they were murdered by those two bastards. But knowing is one thing, proving it is another."

The police found no more graves on Saddleworth Moor and, as the peat became iron-hard with winter, the search was called off. But Douglas Nimmo, true to his reputation, never gave up and never stopped trying to give comfort to Joan Reade and Winnie Johnson. He visited them both regularly to assure them that he and his men were doing everything they could. "I felt so very, very sorry for them," he once said.

Winnie was a regular visitor to her local Longsight police station where Nimmo had given orders that she should always be made welcome and be shown every kindness. By now she had nine children, but the one who occupied her every waking thought was her eldest whom she had not seen since that summer night. "I call in when I'm out shopping and just walk to the CID room," she would say. "Sometimes I take my younger children in with me. I chat to the detectives for about half an hour each visit. It helps a little to talk about Keith. Sometimes I break down and cry, but they are very understanding, always so kind to me."

The day-to-day CID work had to go on and Nimmo, in charge of the detection of crime in two cities, Manchester and its neighbour Salford, was building up a formidable reputation as a crook catcher and a copper not to be trifled with.

One of his more spectacular successes was running the notorious Kray twins off his patch in a fashion that had all the style of an episode from a film or TV script. The Eastend thugs, Reginald and Ronald, had wanted to muscle in on Manchester's thriving night club and casino scene. It was ripe, ready, they decided, for rich pickings and their aim was to set up a protection racket and milk the wealthy club owners who controlled the city's swinging night life.

On 23 September 1966, the Krays and their henchmen stepped off the London train at Manchester's Piccadilly station. In their party was former world heavyweight boxing champion Joe Louis who had, unsuspectingly, been used as a respectable 'cover' for their trip to the North.

The gang had travelled to Manchester on the pretext of accompanying the ex-champion to a fight at Belle Vue Stadium. The Northern detectives, though, knew the real reason for their visit: to begin putting the 'arm' on the city's clubland bosses. And they were waiting for them.

The police operation that clicked into gear that night was spearheaded by Nimmo, Eric Cunningham, co-ordinator of the regional crime squad and other senior detectives, including Detective Inspector Charles Abraham, all of whom had worked together on the Moors case.

They watched every move the gangsters made after their arrival. Less than 24 hours later, in the lounge of the Midland Hotel where the Krays were staying, the brothers looked up as a waiter approached their table with a silver salver. On the tray was a railway timetable and a note bearing a brief message: "*Get out of town.*"

An hour later the gangsters were taking their seats on a train back to London and as it pulled from the station the glowering Krays were waved off by the detectives. Nimmo sucked on his pipe as he and his men walked from Piccadilly and vowed that nobody would get away with trying to sell protection on his patch.

He had beaten the Krays, but he still hadn't cracked Ian Brady and Myra Hindley, who by then had served four months of the life sentences they were given. He went to see them, she in Holloway, he in Durham, to ask them what they knew about Pauline and Keith. Perhaps now there would be a little remorse, some acceptance that nothing they could say could make their fate better or worse. But there were only two words from her: "Ask Ian." And two from him: "Fuck off."

The police chief returned to Saddleworth Moor with a team of men, but it still yielded no clue. The ground in Gorton, in Longsight, was covered again. David Smith returned to the Moor with detectives to try to help. Nothing.

Nimmo's fine career – he investigated more than 100 murders – earned him an MBE in 1969. The following year, by then a grandfather, he retired from the force and became an electricity board security chief. He and his wife Ella later moved to the Lancashire seaside town of Lytham, near Blackpool where he tended his roses and played golf daily until breaking a hip in an accident in 1985.

He became a familiar figure, limping along the promenade with his walking stick, outwardly content, peacefully enjoying his hard-earned retirement. But inwardly he would be haunted for the rest of his days by something he could never forget.

The dreadful pain in the eyes of Joan Reade and Winnie Johnson.

Chapter Three

A MOTHER'S PLEA

13 March, 1986

THE memory of the hate of the woman who had written that still unseen letter to Ian Brady would be impossible to forget. And so would that of what they did to her little girl.

Her clothes had been taken off, she had been made to pose, naked, trembling, whimpering with fear while he took photographs of her. They had, to add to the gratification of their unspeakable lust, tape-recorded her last sounds on earth. Her screams for mercy, pity, help.

"Please, God, help me... I want to see mummy." And the first, and last, time anyone had ever so addressed Ian Brady and Myra Hindley: *"Please, mummy, daddy. Please..."*

She had promised, in her pleading: "I will swear on the Bible." Presumably it was a tearful pledge of silence if they would let her go. How could that innocent little girl have known that that final test of the truth for children would mean nothing to those who had become disciples of the devil?

Slowly, reluctantly, his eyes returned to the envelope. How that little girl with the soft dark curls had pleaded. *"Please, daddy..."*

They had got away with it, he and Myra. And with the others. Or they might have, had it not been for David Smith. But for him, Myra's sister's husband, he might not be *here* today.

David Smith had been 16 when he had made the 18-year-old Maureen pregnant (their baby later died) and married her. He had been good to Smith. Too good, too trusting. He and Myra had taken the Smiths everywhere, even to *their* place. He had introduced him to his books on

37

pornography, torture, sadism. They had even plotted to rob a bank together. Smith had drunk his wine, taken his hospitality. He had been so sure he could trust him, so certain he was ready to become a disciple. So absolutely certain that he had told him he was capable of killing, had killed before and was ready to kill again.

David and Maureen had, in the summer of 1965, also moved from the slums of Gorton to Hattersley, to live in a tower block of flats a few hundred yards away from 16 Wardle Brook Avenue, where Myra's new car, a pale blue Mini Countryman, with folding rear seats, now stood outside. The two couples saw more and more of each other. Smith seemed to be increasingly sharing his views. He had stood, though he had not known it, close to *the graves* when they had taken them to Saddleworth Moor. So Ian Brady, without naming names, names he now tried to blot from his mind, let him into part of his secret.

Smith had not believed him, thought he was playing a game, talking crazy, but Brady had shown him. On the night of 6 October 1965 he proved beyond any doubt to David Smith that he *could* kill. Myra had lured the then 17-year-old Smith to their house on a pretext, just in time for him to witness Brady performing the last brutal, horrifying ritual of his murderous career.

Edward Evans. He had been 17 when Brady and Myra had coaxed him, like the others, into their company. They had taken him from Central Station in Manchester, back to Wardle Brook Avenue and there, with the full connivance of Myra, he had hacked the life from the teenager with an axe, making sure that Smith would see the final death throes of their victim.

But Smith had betrayed them. They had trusted him, allowed him to leave the house with the secret. He had promised to return next day to help them dispose of the body, but it had been the police who next morning came to the door of Number 16. The game was up, and over.

One by one the detectives had uncovered their secrets. The tape recordings, the photographs of Lesley Ann, and the pictures that had pinpointed the graves of their victims.

But they had told the police nothing, he and Myra. Denied everything, through those hours and hours, weeks and weeks of interrogation. And vowed to get that bastard Smith. Even when they found the two bodies they brazened it out.

His mind often returned to their trial, to 1966 when side-by-side they faced justice. She had been so strong then, Myra, so faithful as together they had fought for their liberty and tried to implicate David Smith in the killings. But they hadn't believed them.

May 6, 1966. A date he would never forget.

Ian Brady: Guilty of murdering Edwards Evans. Guilty of murdering Lesley Ann Downey. Guilty of murdering John Kilbride. Myra Hindley: Guilty of murdering Edward Evans. Guilty of murdering Lesley Ann Downey. Not Guilty of murdering John Kilbride. Guilty of harbouring Ian Brady knowing he had killed him.

And the words of the judge: *"I pass the only sentence which the law now allows...life imprisonment."*

After that day they never saw each other again, but they had kept their secrets *about the others.* The names, repeated often by police officers who had visited them in jail, who had searched in vain all those years ago on Saddleworth Moor, swam back to the surface of his mind. *Pauline R... Keith B...* The voices of the detectives: *"We are inquiring about the whereabouts of..."*

For 20 years they had kept their silence about the others. For they had once been so close, he and Myra. He had even wanted to marry her then, if those bastards from the Home Office had allowed it. Marry her! *Her!* Now there was only contempt for the woman who had changed, had spurned his love for the greater love of the freedom she yearned. She had not been prepared, like him, to take her punishment, serve her sentence.

Her professed love for him had cooled during the early years of their imprisonment and finally died. Her only passion was to be free. How she had tried – with religion, with letters to the outside, petitions to the Home Office, even with having a lesbian affair with one of her guards to use her to try an escape. *Silly two-faced bastard*. Yes, she had tried everything, her and that Lord Longford, "silly old fool", even though she knew that *they* would be waiting for her on the outside – the families, those who had sworn to kill her if ever she was freed.

Once more Ian Brady's eyes returned to the letter he said he could not read. He could understand the hatred, the eye-for-an-eye attitude. But *this*, this letter. He shook his head.

He shared the contempt, now, of the families for Myra Hindley, but he had shown her. Each time she had sought her freedom he had had something to say. Like: "I have always accepted that the weight of the crimes *both Myra and I* were convicted of justifies permanent imprisonment, regardless of expressed personal remorse and verifiable change." And, when she was about to take her case to the European Court of Human Rights: "If I revealed what really happened Myra would not get out in a hundred years."

So she was still there, in prison, where she belonged, where she should always stay, where she WOULD always stay.

Ian Brady pushed a thin hand through the now greying hair. He was now 48 years old and no longer a prison inmate, but a mental patient moved, as had been his wish, to a top security hospital, Park Lane in Liverpool.

In prison, as expected – as some had hoped – his life had been tormented by other prisoners who loathed molesters and killers of children and he had chosen to spend most of his sentence in solitary confinement cursing the Home Office, cursing Myra Hindley.

And then there had been the voices. Asking questions about missing children. He believed that his inquisitors were deliberately brainwashing him through the air ducts in his cell. His weight had dropped from a strapping 13 stones to 7 stones 10 pounds while he was in Gartree Prison Leicestershire. "The reduction...was caused by a programme of systematic harrassment, goading and baiting conducted by the Home Office in combination with the withholding of adequate medication," he said.

He told his solicitor Benedict Birnberg in a letter: "The Home Office has been, and still is, piping garbage at me through the air ventilation system, i.e. a continuous series of questions designed to extract information from me about past cases not yet cleared from their books. This has been, and is, keeping me awake till three, four or five in the morning. I haven't been to bed for over a year, but fall asleep from exhaustion in my chair by the window."

He had claimed, too, that his food was being cut down and "tampered with" and had even issued a High Court writ against the Home Office which, he said, was blocking his attempts to get a transfer to a mental hospital.

Finally, in the autumn of 1985, his wish was granted. Doctors found Brady, who had talked of suicide, to be suffering from acute paranoia and a type of schizophrenia.

He picked up the letter. He could not bring himself to read it. He knew of the woman who had written it. He had seen her a long time ago, across the courtroom where he and Myra had first faced their accusers. He remembered the pale, tear-stained face, remembered the anger as she had spat her hate at Myra: *"I'll kill you...I'll kill you."* Yes, the writer of the letter was a woman with every reason to hate, whose life they had destroyed, whose every waking moment from drug-induced sleep cursed their being. Mrs Ann West, the mother of little Lesley Ann Downey.

Brady knew, too, what she wanted and knew the names that would be contained in that letter. They forced their way finally from his tormented brain to his lips. *Pauline Reade. Keith Bennett.*

And Ann West, unbelievably, wanted to see him, to talk to him, face-to-face, about them, to try to help two other mothers in Manchester to find the truth to the excruciatingly painful question that had gnawed at them for a lifetime: where were their children, their daughter, their son? Only two people in all *this* world knew. Ian Brady was one of them.

He had also had a letter from poor Winnie Johnson that

had asked the same thing. This one would say Please help. Please end their suffering. Please, for God's sake.

God. Myra Hindley had turned to Him, but *their* souls had already been surrendered to the devilish evil they created at Gorton, at Hattersley and on Saddleworth Moor.

His hand still shook as he tapped another of the French cigarettes from the white and blue packet. *Pauline Reade, John Kilbride, Keith Bennett, Lesley Ann Downey, Edward Evans*. The names haunted him. And especially now, almost 21 years after they had arrested him. How little they knew. For in the twisted, sick mind of Ian Brady that had kept so many secrets for so long there was much, much more to tell of death.

A new horror story was about to begin.

ANN WEST had made one of the most difficult decisions of her life. The letter to Ian Brady had seemed to be glued to her hand before she eventually pushed it into the post box. God only knew how hard it would be to come face to face and talk to the maniac who had robbed her of her dearest possession, who had taken the life from her beautiful little girl as though it were worthless.

Mrs West is not a strong woman physically. She has bronchial asthma, has had two heart attacks and has survived cancer of the ovaries. I have talked to her many times. She is a pleasant woman of 57 who chats normally and naturally about everyday things. But she laughs only with her mouth. Her eyes betray the deep-rooted, incurable sadness inside, a sadness that replaced the panic of 26 December 1964 when Lesley Ann disappeared from her life.

It is an emotion rivalled only by the rage she feels towards Myra Hindley, the woman she has sworn to kill if ever she is freed. "She is a woman, but where were her motherly instincts when my little girl was pleading for her life?" she once said to me in the living room of the house she shares with her second husband Alan, who has endured the years of pain with her.

The rage swells to fury each time Myra Hindley – or her champion, Lord Longford – makes a move, a plea, towards that hoped-for freedom. Ann West has devoted her life to keeping the murderess she hates more than Brady behind bars.

She had seen, too, the terrible grief of Joan Reade and Winnie Johnson, whose pain of not knowing what had happened to their children had lasted more than twenty times longer than hers. She had tried to comfort them through the organisation she formed, The Murder Victims' Association, but she knew they would only find peace when their daughter or son could be laid to rest in a Christian grave.

Her obsession with watching, through the media, every reported move that Myra Hindley made, had led her to become aware of the cat-and-mouse game that Ian Brady had been playing with her; and he, too, seemed intent on making sure she remained a prisoner for the rest of her life. He was resigned to *his* fate. He had said that he wanted to die in captivity. Was he now ready to tell *all*. And seal the fate of *her*?

Mrs West had applied to the Home Office for permission to see Brady. She was afraid, but her fear was overruled by her hatred for Myra Hindley. "I used to think it would kill me to see him," she said, "but he has said that he could keep *her* in jail for a hundred years if he really spilled the beans. I *must* see him, and try to get him to talk."

And then she posted that letter to her child's murderer, never realising that he would be more afraid of reading it than she had been of sending it.

IAN BRADY later publicly admitted he was afraid to read the letter that Ann West, helped by Alan, had so carefully composed in the hope that it would arouse some emotion – if not compassion, remorse, pity or guilt, then hate for Myra Hindley – in him. He had known for three weeks that she had requested a meeting and that her letter contained the same appeal, but an inbuilt barrier inside his sick mind had closed when he had first been arrested. It had blocked every question about missing children, buried children by the police, by the voices in his head, the "piped garbage" in his cell, for more than 21 years. The names had been hurled at him so often by the police, and mentioned gently the last time, when he was in Gartree, by that new Manchester CID chief. What was his name? Oh yes, *Topping*. There'd been something different about *him*. A quiet determination. He knew he'd be back. But he'd said nothing.

The shield had come down at first when he learned of Ann West's desire to see him and when he had been handed her letter which might have made him recall the words from *The Life and Ideas of the Marquis de Sade* that had been his bible. *"The only punishment which a murderer should be condemned to is that which he risks from the friends or the family of the man he has killed."*

But eventually he had been unable to stop his thoughts returning to Manchester, to Saddleworth Moor, to the children he had killed. And to Myra Hindley. Like Ann West, he monitored her every move, noted her every utterance, like that in a recent magazine interview. In it she had said she would be willing to wait until she was 80 if only she could get out of jail. And: "Only an idiot, or someone who's afraid to be free wouldn't want to. I still want to enjoy some freedom."

ONLY AN IDIOT. SOMEONE WHO'S AFRAID TO BE FREE. The words struck insultingly, infuriatingly, close to home. Right, Myra. Brady picked up his pen.

And on the *Nine O'Clock News*, on Friday, 14 March 1986 there was an item that made Ann West's heart pound painfully. The BBC had had a letter from Ian Brady saying he was prepared to meet her.

"I PLEAD with him and beg him to help and reveal what he knows," Ann West told her interviewers, painfully aware that her little girl had once pleaded with him and begged him to no avail. She knew she would need every reserve of her strength to come face to face with Brady. It was a terrifying prospect, but she was determined to go through with it.

She knew of the great physical change in Ian Brady, whose cold grey eyes, set in the handsome, high cheek-boned face of a young man had once been upon her in a courtroom as she sobbed her hate at Myra Hindley. And of the mental change in the man, whose move to hospital – "more like a Holiday Inn" declared the critics – meant he was never now compelled to see anyone.

Lord Longford, though, continued to visit him and reported a change for the better. "He looked like a scarecrow in prison, but now he has put on a lot of weight and is looking better."

Doctors at Park Lane, however, were more concerned with his mental condition. He was undoubtedly in a state of growing agitation at the prospect of the meeting. They did not feel it would be in his best interests, and it is unlikely that Brady had taken much persuading to see their point of view: that the encounter with the mother of one of his victims would be unwise. Would he have been able to go through with the confrontation? Or had it been an exercise aimed at jolting, scaring Myra Hindley, making her believe he was ready to tell, to begin spilling *their* secrets? *Who's an idiot? Who's afraid?*

Though she had dreaded it, the calling off of the meeting dismayed Ann West, while intensifying her resolve to keep Hindley in jail. Four days later she was standing outside the heavy gates of Cookham Wood Prison, near Rochester, Kent where the murderess was serving the last few weeks of the twentieth year of her life sentence, trying to rally support for her campaign.

It was not easy, on that drizzly March day, to get signatures for the massive petition she had built up over the years. Most of the people living in the area were the families of prison officers who were reluctant to get involved. Mrs West and her husband returned to Manchester, having at least made six paragraphs in the *Daily Mail* for their presence at Cookham Wood. Every little helped.

But ten days later there came a development that was to make far more than six paragraphs in another newspaper. *Sunday Today* reported that Myra Hindley had "confessed" to *another* murder – that of a 16-year-old girl. *"She's on the Moors with the others...and they'll never find her,"* shouted the headline. According to the story by Author Fred Harrison, the girl had been killed by Brady and Hindley. Miss Doreen Wright, now 55, a former nursing sister at Holloway, where Myra had begun her sentence, had claimed that the outburst had been made in a fit of rage, 20 years ago. The former nurse had confirmed her allegation in a sworn statement.

Why, asked the cynics, had Miss Wright kept her silence for so long? She had thought, she said, that she was bound by the Official Secrets Act. Hmm, said the cynics, including Lord Longford. "Absolute nonsense," he declared. "I have seen her (Myra) about seventy times over the past 17 years and on not one occasion has she ever made any such admission about further killings." But she wouldn't to *him*, would she? It was argued. She always put on her best face for him. He was her Public Relations man, arguing her case for liberty. The police said, as they always said, that the claim would be carefully investigated, just like any other piece of information.

Meanwhile, that night, there was food for tortured thought for Ian Brady. And, on the Lancashire coast, the retired Nimmo told my colleague David Graham that he was still haunted by the unclosed files of the two missing youngsters he had left behind and by the thought of what their families must be going through.

There is no doubt that the 16-year-old girl that Myra Hindley was alleged to have referred to was a name on the file stamped indelibly in Nimmo's mind: *Pauline Reade*.

Her brother Paul, now 38 – almost 23 years after he had

last seen his sister in the pink dance dress – was saying: "I beg the authorities...please take those two monsters back to the Moors to find my sister's grave and end our agony."

It was an appeal that, though he would never have believed it, would one day, not far away, be heeded.

Ian Brady and Myra Hindley would soon return to hell.

Chapter Four

BRADY'S REMORSE

THE spring flowers were budding, bursting and blooming outside. The air was filled with the songs of the birds, uncaged, mating in freedom as he had mated with her so many springs ago. Ian Brady's mind was once more on their courting ground, and their killing fields, Gorton, Hattersley, Saddleworth. And on the young people whose lives they had taken to satisfy an obscene hunger far greater than any love they felt for each other. The high forehead furrowed in concentration as his pen moved slowly across the notepaper.

"Re letters from Mrs West and the mother of Keith Bennett. Although I have been given them I have not been able to bring myself to read them." The pen paused. The memory, the voices, perhaps the screams, were still there. "I have been afraid to read them. Understand?

"I have to keep mental blocks tightly shut and keep control. The authorities have refused Mrs West's requests to visit me...I can't say how it would have worked out if the meeting had taken place. Remorse for my part in this and other matters is axiomatic, painfully deep."

Now for the never-to-be-missed opportunity of turning the knife in Myra Hindley. "But I despise useless, empty words and prefer positive action to balance part of the past, i.e. the Braille I have done for schools this past 18 years and which the authorities here are making it difficult for me to do."

He sent the letter to his usual "post office," the BBC in London and it was read on the *Six O' Clock News* on Wednesday, 9 April 1986. *He* had said to the world that *he* was sorry, so sorry "for *my* part in this and *other matters.*" The key words had been chosen to act like rapier thrusts to Myra.

Would she, too, now make a public declaration of

remorse? That would amount to an admission, 20 years after she had told the jury she was Not Guilty. And what would she say about the *other matters*?

Brady had once more put the ball in her court in the one-sided game he had been playing with her, for 14 years, ever since she had spurned his love in her desire to be free, and had stopped writing to him and told Lord Longford: "I find it virtually impossible to recapture even a shred of my previous feelings for him. I wish to put him out of my life as totally as I do all the unhappy, destructive and Godless aspects of my past life with him, and I must admit that I rarely ever think of him now."

The words had stung painfully and Ian Brady had had all the time in the world to weigh them. A lifetime to plot his revenge.

In the secure hospital Brady had made just one friend – a kindred spirit, murderer and rapist Colin Chapman, to whom he first began speaking during group therapy sessions. They held long conversations, speaking together in whispers, discussing, it was said, their crimes. Would Brady have been confiding in Chapman about *the secrets* he had until now shared only with Myra Hindley. About *the others*? If only the still-frustrated Doug Nimmo could have been a fly on the wall...

But now, another policeman was waiting in the wings to renew an investigation that had begun when he was a young bobby on the sidelines. He wanted to talk to Myra Hindley about those "other matters," about two missing children. His name was Peter Topping, the new head of Greater Manchester CID. And he was about to unlock the secrets of death.

★　　★　　★

MYRA HINDLEY was now almost 44. She had spent nearly half her life in prison. Those who visited her would shake their heads in disbelief, she looked so *young*. Unlike Ian Brady, whose body and mind had degenerated, she actually appeared to be more youthful than the hard-faced peroxide blonde whose features had first leered from the front pages of the newspapers in 1966. Now it was a face that was softer, prettier and framed with auburn tinted hair. A face that had defied time and was ready – if only they would let her – to take its place among young people in the world outside, as if the last 20 years had been but a slight pause.

But she would be 48 before her next review for parole. Four more long, long years. She had begged, pleaded, petitioned, "rediscovered" her religion, tried to show the world she had changed and was ready to rejoin it.

After all that, though, one baffling, frustrating, inescapable fact remained. The public relations exercise had failed. It was Ian Brady who was more *respected* – if ever that word could be applied to either of them – in the eyes of the public. Where was she going wrong?

Cookham Wood Prison, 250 miles from the institution where Brady now lived was, unlike Holloway where she had started her sentence, a modern environment. It's cells were centrally heated, there was colour TV, gardens, disco dancing once a week and a number of women, denied the company of men, willing to share their bodies. Her cell had flowered curtains with matching bedspread, religious pictures on the walls, and a crucifix to which she prayed – usually for her freedom

She had always kept her silence, denied everything, told the police nothing and had said to her close friend Carol O'Callaghan in a letter: "I couldn't make statements regarding something I know nothing of..." And of Brady's insinuations: "Whatever he had to say, regardless of any allegations he might make, I could only do as I've always done: deny and dissociate myself from them. If he was believed, there was nothing I could do. My conscience is clear whether I'm believed or not."

Had Myra Hindley's life followed the pattern of her Gorton contemporaries, with a husband, children, shopping, cleaning, washing, ironing, caring, loving, she would not have had the time to dwell upon the one theme that occupied almost her every moment. As the girls she had grown up with dreamed of a pools win, she dreamed, every sleeping and waking minute, of the lives that they had.

She had started to write her life story in the quiet solitude of her cell – God, what a seller *that* would be when...if...she got out – and her mind was back in Manchester where it had all begun. The names of the victims swam in her brain. Which one had it been that had roused more hate, more anger, more public feeling than any other? She *knew*, she felt the rage of the mother who said she would find her, kill her, if ever she set foot outside jail. The tear-stained face beneath the soft dark curls, the voice begging in her bedroom in Hattersley, returned from that Boxing Day of 22 years ago. *"Please, mummy..."*

Myra had been ashamed when, after her arrest, the police had played back to her the tape recording she and Brady had made of the little girl's last words. That was on record. And so was her voice, in duet with Lesley Ann Downey, hers saying: *"Shut up, or I'll forget myself and hit you one."*

That tape had been the catalyst, the thing that had damned her. Inescapable evidence that she had taken Lesley Ann to the hell she shared with Ian Brady and that, in her own words at her trial, her behaviour had been "indefensible, cruel and criminal." She had, of course, always denied killing Lesley Ann, and had tried, unsuccessfully, to implicate the innocent David Smith. But she could never deny being there, in her bedroom, with Lesley Ann. The tape recording said it all.

Ian had switched on the tape recorder. They had listened to it afterwards. The recording had been made for their mutual gratification, a memento of another of their murderous conquests. But it was also a memento of their mutual *guilt*. The cunning, crafty bugger.

She wanted to hear it again, to listen in her cell, to every word, every scream. Was there any way, she asked Lord Longford the next time he visited her, of getting that tape recording? She was sure that, if she heard it again, she could "explain" her behaviour. For she now had a way with words, a way of sculpting, shaping them, thanks to her long studies through the Open University which had gained her a Bachelor of Arts degree. There was, of course, no way that tape would ever be released, especially to her. In any case, however skilful with words, whoever could find an ambiguity, another meaning, for sentences like: *"Shut up or I'll forget myself and hit you one...?"*

Yes, Ian Brady had "stitched her" with that tape recording. To think she had loved him so much. How could a woman fall so completely, hopelessly for him the way she had done?

There was something, though, that Myra Hindley could not know, something she would never have believed possible. There were other girls in the life of Ian Brady.

★　　★　　★

THEY would not even have been born on that summer night when Pauline Reade took her last footsteps to death. They would have only been babies when the shock and horror of the Moors Murders reverberated around the world. But two girls, around the same age as Myra Hindley had been *then*, had formed a bizarre attachment to the man in the secure mental hospital.

One of them was 22, red haired and beautiful. She was a student in history, English and psychology and had begun writing to him in 1983 after being put in touch with him by Lord Longford as "someone who might be able to help me in my university studies in moral philosophy and sociology." She was also, I have little doubt, infatuated by him.

Whatever the basis, the reason for their friendship, whatever the relationship, Ian Brady was said to have written no fewer than 150 letters to her – one a week – during the three years since their introduction. She had also visited the gaunt, tormented man, old enough to be her father, at Park Lane. Had that first meeting of the eyes, his cold, hers warm, captivated her as they had Myra Hindley?

There was another vying for his affections. She was 21, also red-haired, though hers was dyed and cut in the style of a punk. Punk? Teddy Boys were giving way to Mods and Rockers, then they to the long-haired khaftan-wearing flower people, hippies, when Ian Brady and Myra Hindley were shut off from the changing world outside. Myra had changed with the styles. But Brady hadn't.

Perhaps that was the fascination. A man, his short hair still swept back, caught in a time warp, a prisoner in mind and body, of the swinging and, with his contribution, shocking sixties. James Dean, growing old.

The second girl had started writing to him while she was still at school, as part of a project, and it had not stopped there. During their correspondence, Ian Brady had suggested that the two girls should meet. And they did, on his direction, on a boat trip down the River Clyde, swopping lines from his letters, exchanging confidences about their fascination for the man whose deeds had chilled their parents.

They were two girls sharing an infatuation for a man whose Svengali-like influence, magnetism, had lured another, so long ago. And captured her soul to hand to the Devil on Saddleworth Moor.

The first girl had not told her mother of her association with Ian Brady. She would never understand. Nor had her boyfriend. "Goodbye", he had said, when she told him that the Moors Murderer had stepped into her life. She told no-one else, for fear of becoming an outcast among her fellow-students.

It was not until May of 1986 – coinciding, ironically, exactly, with the twentieth anniversary of Brady's life sentence – that the Press had got wind of the relationship. "The Girl Who Loves Ian Brady," yelled the front page of *The Star*, whose exclusive had been triggered by a theft. The letters from Ian Brady – "love letters" – had been stolen from the girl's bed-sitter in Edinburgh. And, it was said, they were being touted around Fleet Street by two men whose asking price was £30,000

The theft of the letters was reported to the police. The

press clamoured for more information. The girl hid from the reporters and issued a statement through her solicitor. She insisted that she had visited Brady only once, in the presence of a hospital officer. "I was surprised to find a sad and broken man," she said. "I felt sympathy for him and continued to write to him. He clearly valued our correspondence. I enjoyed our correspondence...but would like to say that the newspaper reports have exaggerated it into something it never was." And, said her solicitor, she did not see the correspondence as an exchange of "love letters."

The mother of the other girl was saying: "I know she has been writing to him, but they are not romantically linked...just pen pals." Yes, she said, her daughter had "taken a lot of stick" for writing to Ian Brady. And a neighbour had asked the girl to leave a party at his home after discovering that she had corresponded with the killer.

Ian Brady had clearly fascinated the girls with his knowledge of everything from philosophy to Russian literature, gathered during his studies in prison. And despite the deteriorating condition of his mind and body there was still the ability to bewitch, the magnetism that had drawn Myra Hindley when she had been their age. Though evil had obviously lain in the heart of Myra and he had released it, he had also brought out the tenderness that had remained after their arrest, after the realisation that she might never see him again.

"*Dearest Ian, hello my little hairy Girklechin...I had a beautifully tender dream about you last night and awoke feeling safe and secure, thinking I was in the harbour of your arms. Even when I realised I wasn't the thought of your presence remained with me, leaving me tranquilly calm and strong.*" The words, written by Myra just before their first Christmas in jail, in 1966, were those of a woman totally, helplessly in love.

"*Each day that passes I miss you more and more. You are the only thing that keeps my heart beating, my only reason for living. Without you what does life mean?*

54

Nothing, absolutely nothing. Freedom without you means nothing too. I've got one interest in life and that's you. We had six short but precious years together, six years of memories to sustain us until we're together again, to make dreams realities..."

How her feelings had changed. Now she used sweet words only to those who could help her alone to be free. Her latest appeal had been to the European Commission of Human Rights in Strasbourg, an eloquently couched claim that she had been imprisoned for too long. Her treatment had been inhuman, degrading, and she had suffered physical and mental effects. But the 17 commissioners disagreed. The complaints were "manifestly ill-founded," they said. "We find no evidence that the applicant has suffered inhuman or degrading treatment."

Myra Hindley was in a no-win situation. Her efforts to win round the public, to show them she had changed had, in fact, alienated her even more from those she had hoped to impress. Even when, that summer, she had taken part in a sponsored six-mile run for Sport Aid to help starving children in Africa, the newspaper headlines reported: "*Fiend* Myra runs for famine children!"

The decision-makers in Whitehall were unimpressed by her attempts to appear the lesser of the two evil people and impeccable Home Office sources had told my colleague, political editor of *The Star*, Anthony Smith, that she could forget any hopes of freedom for a long, long time. They had pored over confidential background and the case notes made by policemen in the 1960s and since. They were also mindful of one conclusion made by some of the officers who spent hours in her company: that she was the more dominant of the evil partnership. And of the chilling suspicion that she might even have encouraged Brady to torture and kill.

Smith reported that the Home Office had noted that Myra had never helped the police in their inquiries of where other bodies might be found and that she had spent recent years trying to explain and minimise her role rather than expressing her full remorse for what she had done. A senior source told him: "It is a certainty that it will be a long, long time before she will be considered for release. Where there is a well of poison and evil, as in case, the only way to get it out of the system is to confess and bring everything out into the open. This, conspicuously, this woman has failed to do. Indeed, she has shown herself to be the arch manipulator...and she is pulling the wool over nobody's eyes."

It was time for a change of tactics and Myra Hindley had, lying in front of her that November day, a device that could be used to her advantage, a lever to show *her* 'remorse.'

A ghost had just stepped from her past. A letter from Winnie Johnson.

★　　★　　★

"DEAR Miss Hindley. I am sure I am one of the last people you would ever have expected to receive a letter from. I am the mother of Keith Bennett who went missing, no one knows where, on June 16, 1964. As a woman I am sure you can envisage the nightmare I have lived with day and night, 24 hours a day, since then. Not knowing whether my son is alive or dead, whether he ran away or was taken away, is literally a living hell, something which you no doubt have experienced during your many years locked in prison. My letter to you now is written out of desperation and faint hope: desperation because I know that, for so many years, neither you nor Ian Brady has admitted knowing anything about my son's disappearance, and hope that Christianity has softened your soul so much that you would never any longer knowingly condemn someone to permanent purgatory.

"Please, I beg of you, tell me what happened to Keith. My heart tells me you know and I, on bended knees, am begging you to end this torture and finally put my mind at rest. Besides asking for your pity, the only other thing I can say is that by helping me you will doubtless help yourself because all those people who have harboured so much hate against you and prevented your being released a long time ago would have no reason left to harbour their hate. By telling me what happened to Keith you would be announcing loudly to the world that you really HAVE turned into the caring, warm person that Lord Longford speaks of. I am a simple woman, I work in the kitchens of Christie's Hospital. It has taken me five weeks labour to write this letter because it is so important to me that it is understood by you for what it is, a plea for help. Please, Miss Hindley, help me.''

Myra Hindley read the letter, in her cell at Cookham Wood, again. And again. Particularly the lines... *''by helping me you will doubtless help yourself.''*

And ''...*you would be announcing loudly to the world that you really HAVE turned into the caring, warm person that Lord Longford speaks of.''*

On Monday, 17 November 1986, 21 years, one week and three days after a policeman's knock on her council house door brought her evil to an end, Myra Hindley began to help the police with their inquiries.

Chapter Five

MYRA TELLS

THERE had once been an age gap of a generation between Myra Hindley and her police inquisitors. In those days she had tossed her head in defiance, stared them straight in the eye and denied everything.

The man now facing her was different, slim, softly spoken, with the look and air of a bank manager or an accountant. But he, too, was a policeman. Detective Chief Superintendent Peter Topping. At 47, he was only three years older than her and nearly two years younger than Ian Brady. It was a jolt, a reminder of the 20 years that had passed and that policemen look more youthful the older you get.

Topping had been a bobby on the beat in those far-off days when hard-bitten police chiefs like Arthur Benfield, Joe Mounsey and Doug Nimmo had been the interrogators. He knew how difficult their job had been in trying to break down the barrier of silence with which the murderess had surrounded herself. He also felt that there was probably little hope of succeeding where they had failed.

He was a different breed of policeman from the grizzled old-timers, far less of an extrovert and, during his climb up the ranks to head of operations of Greater Manchester CID had, sneered some, spent too many hours behind a desk. Peter Topping cared little for bar-top chat, preferring to spend his spare time either swimming, cycling or jogging, or with his wife and two grown-up children in his Manchester suburban home.

He shared, however, the desire of his predecessors to close once and for all the files on Pauline Reade and Keith Bennett, the yellowed dossiers he had opened on his desk more than a year earlier, soon after taking up his new post.

That year, 1985, there had, in Topping's words, been "renewed public awareness" of the Moors Murders. For the twentieth anniversary of the arrest of Brady and

Hindley had awakened in a whole new generation, the shocking realisation of just why there was such fierce, angry determination by its elders to keep the murderers caged for the rest of their lives.

There had also been newspaper reports of alleged confessions by Ian Brady. The public wanted to know what was being done. Was there any evidence to connect Brady and Hindley with the disappearances and almost certain deaths of Pauline Reade and Keith Bennett? The Director of Public Prosecutions wanted answers, too.

Topping examined the papers, the case notes that had been held by Cheshire CID and had spearheaded the original investigation. He listened, as Benfield, Mounsey, Nimmo and other senior detectives had once listened, to David Smith, whose torment will never end, and who continued to insist that the two people he had known so well had claimed other victims. Smith had gone with me to Greater Manchester police headquarters, expecting a polite indifference, but Peter Topping and his men clung to his every syllable.

Throughout the summer of 1986, though no-one knew it, the police had been paying visits to Saddleworth Moor, using specially-trained sheep dogs to re-examine the place where, two decades earlier, there had been so much activity. This time it was a low-key operation, with the officers dressed as shepherds to merge with their surroundings.

It had been, as one senior detective remarked later, the best kept secret in Greater Manchester police. But the low profile nature of the investigation also meant that Topping could not carry out the methodical grid-pattern system, marking out search areas, he knew was really necessary and possibly, eventually, inevitable.

The Detective Chief Superintendent had also visited Ian Brady, then in Gartree Prison before his move to the mental hospital. He had as usual had nothing to say.

Now, more than a year later, Topping was sitting opposite Myra Hindley in Cookham Wood Prison. Behind his pleasant, mild manner though, was a feeling, a burning inside that Doug Nimmo would have recognised. For, during his inquiries, Peter Topping had also seen that awful, soul-disturbing torture in the sad faces of Joan Reade and Winnie Johnson.

Now, though he expected little to come from the meeting, Topping was confronting Myra because, as he was to say later in one of his carefully thought-out, painstakingly-worded statements, "she had indicated a willingness to cooperate with my inquiries."

What happened next behind those prison walls as he looked into the eyes of the Moors Murderess was to send his pulse racing.

The reluctant jailbird started to sing...

THE two detectives, Peter Topping and his colleague Inspector Geoffrey Knupfer, who had travelled to Kent with him, glanced at each other. In the eyes of most other men there would have been a gleam of triumph, but those of Peter Topping retained the soft, understanding look that accommodated the gaze of Myra Hindley.

She was nodding her head. Yes, she was willing to cooperate. What could she do?

Topping gently pressed on, his voice warm, gentle with encouragement. They would come back next day with maps of Saddleworth Moor, and photographs she had not seen for a long, long time, pictures she and Ian had taken for their tartan-backed album that had provided the damning evidence against them at their trial.

On Tuesday, 18 November Topping spent almost four hours with Myra, poring over maps of the Pennine landscape and showing her photographs that, at first sight, appeared to portray a young couple in love, at play. But these were pictures he knew could have a grim significance, just like the photographs discovered by detectives in 1965, that had acted as pointers to the graves of the Moors Murderers' young victims.

The unbelievable was happening. Myra, peering intently from behind the spectacles she now had to wear for reading, was nodding, pointing to spots on the map, to places, like Hollin Brow Knoll, where she and her lover had shared their ghastly secrets. Yes, she had been there, and there, with Ian Brady.

Was there a mist on the spectacles as she took them off to wipe them with her handkerchief? Had a tear been shed for a lost youth, a lost love, a lost soul?

She looked at Topping. Yes, tears were beginning to stain her face. She felt so sorry, she said for the families of the two missing children. So very sorry, troubled, at the thought of a mother who had a child not properly buried. That was why she was crying, she said. She had been so moved by the letter from Winnie Johnson.

She issued a personal statement through her solicitor Michael Fisher: "I received a letter, the first ever, from the mother of one of the missing children and this has caused me enormous distress. I have agreed to help the police in any way possible and have today identified, from photographs and maps, places that I know were of particular interest to Ian Brady, some of which I visited with him. In spite of a 22-year passage of time, I have searched my heart and memory and given whatever help I can give to the police. I'm glad at long last to have been given this opportunity and I will continue to do all that I can."

And then, once more, she was unable to resist another appeal: "I hope that one day people will be able to forgive the wrong I have done and know the truth of what I have and have not done. But for now I want the police to be able to conclude their inquiries, so ending public speculation and the private anguish of those directly involved."

Outside the prison her solicitor told the waiting pressmen: "I saw it happening when I was with her. She was in a state about that letter. She had got to do something about it. I genuinely believe that she was greatly moved by the letter and that she wanted to assist the police for genuine reasons and wasn't thinking in the back of her mind that this would help her to be released one day."

Someone asked a question then that made Mr Fisher shake his head at the mere suggestion. Would Myra

Hindley be taken to the moors to help to search?

"I would have thought that that was completely out of the question," he said. "I think in view of the information she has been able to give to the police today that it won't be necessary – and neither do I think it would be permitted by the Home Office."

No one pressed him further. He was right. The very idea of her returning to her killing grounds really was too far-fetched to contemplate any more.

Meanwhile, back in Manchester, Winnie Johnson, now 53, whose anguish had tormented her for 23 years, was saying: "Never, in my wildest dreams, did I think that *she* would answer me." Tiny, homely, bespectacled Mrs Johnson, the sandy hair now grey, still could not grasp the full significance of the development. "I don't know whether to believe her or not, I don't know why I should trust her."

She had prayed for the breakthrough, but now it had come it made her shiver with the full realisation of its consequences. "It's such a dreadful feeling that..." She paused, whispered... "that I might soon know the truth. I feel numb."

She had spent three months writing to Brady, begging him, but had never received a reply. She had learned that her letters had lain unopened. *He* had been too frightened of their contents. But Myra Hindley hadn't...

Winnie, now living two miles from the house of too many painful memories of Keith, found it difficult to sleep that night, her mind flooded once more with the pictures of the little lad in the wire-rimmed National Health spectacles. Of that pavement where she had kissed him for the last time. *"See you tomorrow, mam..."*

There had been no tomorrow for Keith Bennett, but he had never died in the memory of his mother. And Winnie knew that would happen if, when, the black Pennine peat 20 miles away yielded another of its dark secrets. He would still be in her thoughts every day. But, perhaps, in fewer of her nightmares.

The eccentric Lord Longford, as always, pressed home

the advantage for the woman he had championed for 17 years. "I think this is a breakthrough in the sense that the public will now realise that she is a good woman," he declared. "If she was a character in a Dostoyevsky novel she would be the heroine. I think Myra will be released from prison. It would be a terrible thing if she was not. She is still in her forties and if she was not released it would show cowardice on the part of the Government and keep alive the hatred towards her.

"I think the Home Secretary (Mr Douglas Hurd) is a good man and will do the right thing. Myra had a change of heart years ago. What people will not believe is that she feels remorse and has done for many years. People cannot get it into their heads."

Yes, he agreed, in helping the police, Myra could now be accused of other crimes. "But I don't think this has lessened her chances of release. In fact I hope it has improved them."

The elderly peer rounded on the newspapers who had described her as "the most evil woman in the country". He said: "That is such balderdash. Anyone who says that should be certified and have psychiatric treatment. I hope that public opinion will realise this is a real live woman and not some sort of fiend, as portrayed by the tabloids, who are so absolutely filthy and wicked."

Filthy and wicked? Could not that be a more apt description for the woman for whose freedom he was fighting? asked some. Ann West was not taken in, she said. "I don't think that woman has ever changed. Why did she wait all these years before speaking up?" Ann, and many others, concluded that the "remorse" was just another part of the public relations exercise. Myra Hindley had been clever and never, confirmed Mr Topping, given the impression that she was involved in the killings.

Myra, for the first time, had smashed the ball into Brady's court. And the police were going back to Saddleworth Moor.

THE headlines returned to the newspapers, in the same bold, black print that had dominated the front pages 21 years earlier. For no murder story this century has caught the imagination and anger of Britain such as that of Ian Brady and Myra Hindley. "EVIL MYRA TELLS ALL", screamed the banner of *The Star*, like every other popular newspaper reflecting the views of its readers that, whatever she said or did, she would always be "Evil Myra".

It was also clear that this was an opinion shared by people in high places. We learned that the Director of Public Prosecutions had flatly refuted any suggestion that an amnesty, under which neither would face further murder charges, should be granted to the couple. There would be no deals struck with the Moors Murderers.

That day police made the final preparations for the resumed search of the Moor, placing cones along the winding A635 between the village of Greenfield and the Yorkshire town of Holmfirth, a road that had been taken so many times, so long ago by Brady and Hindley. They wanted to keep away sightseers whom they knew would invade the area in their hundreds with a curiosity that had been unabated for 21 years.

Just what had Myra Hindley pointed out to Topping and his men? Her lawyer had said: "She believes it likely that bodies will be found." What secrets had she finally divulged? There was a quiet confidence about the CID chief, who would now be seeking permission from the Department of Health to interview Ian Brady.

Doug Nimmo, the dogged, dedicated detective whose greatest desire, for the sake of two dreadfully tormented mothers, was to find the remains of their children would never know of the breakthrough. For, just a few weeks before Myra Hindley broke her silence and spilled out the words he had longed to hear, he died at his retirement home on the Lancashire coast.

Chapter Six

THE NEW SEARCH

SLOWLY the coach rounded the bend, the driver slipping down a gear to negotiate the tortuous climb. The grass by the roadside was growing sparser, browner, the air outside more chill, and a mist was gathering, thickening, until it became a white mantle, a freezing, mocking shroud. As if to hide death.

In the valley below a wintry sun was still shining, brightening the grey, Pennine stone of the cottages, tinting the few remaining leaves on the silver birches to a bright copper. The light had been left behind as we climbed up the twisting moorland road, the A635, east of Manchester, towards a place that, to many of my travelling companions, had until then been just a name on a map or in the yellowed newspaper cuttings in their pockets. Saddleworth Moor.

The sun was blotted from view as we crept beneath the outer edges of the mantle which allowed only the crumbling dry-stone walls with their rusting barbed wire to be seen. The ravine that had yawned below us was now filled, like a huge lake, with the swirling mist, as if by smoke from the fires of hell, yet as icy as the finger of death.

More than 100 of us had gathered that morning in a car park near the old clock tower of the market hall in the former cotton town of Stalybridge, on the edge of Greater Manchester. Ironically, it had been there where, 21 years earlier, the police station had taken the frantic telephone call from the terrified David Smith that had brought the evil game of the Moors Murderers to an end. It was now the setting-out point for the Press, returning to witness a search for bodies on Saddleworth Moor for the first time since 1965, instigated by the most infamous woman in Britain.

The police had insisted that they should provide the

transport to take us and had laid on three coaches to accommodate the pressmen, few of whom I recognised as being the "originals", those of us who, so long ago, had covered the story when it first broke.

An old friend Brian Crowther from the *Daily Mirror* was there, a little rounder and balder than the young man I had known then. Neither of us had ever thought we would be going back to *that* place in our middle age.

We climbed aboard one of the coaches and I sat down next to my *Star* colleague, reporter Ian Trueman. He was 29 and, I reflected, would have been just eight years old when the first headline of the world's longest-running murder story was written. God, I thought, I was old enough to be his father. The same age as Ian Brady, and still haunted by Myra Hindley.

The coach swung away from the town centre, past the Victorian council buildings, and sharp right onto Wakefield Road, the A635, the route taken so many times a generation ago by a white Mini-Traveller carrying Ian Brady and Myra Hindley...and sometimes a passenger. Past the rows of terraced houses, stretching either side of the road in the ribbon development of the early part of the century, through the tiny township of Mossley, with its brass bands and woollen mills, the buildings becoming fewer, with brick-built town houses being replaced by stone cottages.

Greenfield. The sign of the last village before the long climb to the Pennine plateau, past the Clarence pub on the left, whose sanctuary we, and the policemen, had sought as a relief from it all. And, yes, further on, on the right, it was still there, the red roadside phone box where we had pressed Button A with frozen fingers to file the first words of the story of Saddleworth Moor.

Now past rambling Crowther's Farm, the last building, the final link with civilisation before The Place. The house where young David Crowther, now a 31-year-old father, had had nightmares after he realised, at the age of ten, what the policemen were searching for up that winding road from his lonely home.

The sun slipped away and the mist came down like a blanket, as we climbed higher, nosing around the metal crash barriers until the coach crunched to a halt on the roadside gravel, 1600 feet above sea level, at a spot where the Mini had once stopped; where Ian and Myra had drunk wine. And made love. And performed their last ghastly rituals.

The door slid open and we stepped outside into the white mist. It was freezing, just as it had been 21 years ago when I had last been there to report on a police hunt. And upon dreadful discoveries. We shivered, zipped up our anoraks and stepped from the hard gravel onto the thick, squelching peat, tufted with wet, brown grass.

It was Thursday, 20 November 1986 when I set foot again on Saddleworth Moor, 21 years and one month after an earlier generation of policemen had found the bodies of Lesley Ann Downey and John Kilbride, lying in shallow graves 373 yards apart on opposite sides of the road. Lesley's naked body had been just out of sight of the road, close to an outcrop of rocks known as Hollin Brow Knoll. Near her feet were her royal blue coat, pink cardigan, red and green tartan skirt and a tiny string of white beads that had been a present from her brother Terry. The remains of John – his trousers pulled down to mid-thigh, his underpants rolled into a band and knotted at the back – had been discovered close to where we now stood, the sharp, icy air biting our faces, penetrating our clothing.

Around us, unseen for the mist, was a vast landscape of hills and valleys, rocks and ravines, a place with names like Wildcat Moor, Wessenden Head and Shiny Brook. A place steeped in legends of fear and death.

The area was haunted, said the folklore, with the spirits of dead children, some of whom died from overwork in the valley's woollen mills and had been buried at Greenfield. Ghosts of other children were, according to the local history books, "heard screaming on wild, dark nights in winter". And, it was said, "the little people, the devil's childen", snatched babies from their cradles. They were tales, born of an age of superstition, in another century when, fearful of the evil, the villagers would whisper: *"The Devil's children always have the Devil's work..."*

We now knew that Ian Brady and Myra Hindley had been tainted by that evil and chosen this, of all places, as the altar for the sacrifices of their unspeakable, ungodly deeds.

The last time I had been there, reporters and photographers had travelled to the scene in cars such as Ford Anglias, Hillman Minxes, Mark 1 Cortinas and Morris Minors, to report the findings and then file their stories from Greenfield.

How different the mode of operation was now, with the journalists using portable phones and the senior policemen, no more in overcoats, trilby hats and black wellington boots, but now looking more equipped for a winter sports holiday. This time, the body-searchers were not a line-up of young bobbies, using prodding sticks, raising them to their nostrils, seeking that dreadful tell-tale smell of putrefication. Now the hunters were specially-trained dogs, panting rapidly, with lolling pink tongues, their breath steaming in the cold air.

There were eight of them – Butch, Rebel, Pip, Winston, Bob, Jan and a couple of Sabres, Alsatians, Labradors and Collies who had been trained to detect human remains; remains, the police had been told by forensic experts, that could have been preserved by the peat. Around us, huge areas had been marked out with red flags and white tape, stretches of moorland that had been pointed out to Topping on the photographs by Myra Hindley.

Four areas, each 150 by 100 yards, had been sectioned off. The dogs were to be taken to each one. The area to which they kept returning would pinpoint the spot to be searched.

A man in a bright red ski jacket broke the gloom. Peter Topping faced the pressmen and the TV cameras to tell us he was prepared to be patient. "If we don't have success in the next few weeks we won't be disappointed," he said. "We won't give up." The pattern of the search had been decided before he saw Myra Hindley. "But as a result of seeing her we are much more optimistic that we are in the right area." And Topping had another plan, something he was keeping to himself then. But, we were soon to find out that the Home Secretary was considering an astonishing, almost unthinkable request from the detective.

To take Myra back to Saddleworth Moor.

★   ★   ★

FOR the first time since that spring day in 1966 when the cell door clanged shut behind Myra Hindley in Holloway Prison, a Home Secretary was giving serious thought to letting her out into the world. Peter Topping, backed by his Chief Constable, the controversial, deeply-religious Mr James Anderton, had asked for the murderess to be given three days to return to the Moor to help pinpoint the search spot more accurately; to see if she could remember, after almost a quarter of a century, the places she had 'visited' with Ian Brady.

It was an extremely difficult decision for the Home Secretary, Douglas Hurd, to make. He was fully aware that the woman in his charge, for whom he must take total responsibility, was the most hated in the land and that controversy surrounded every move she made. He had learned that, in her talks with Topping, she had agreed to return to Saddleworth. He knew, also, that there would be many who would question her motives.

The Star's political editor, Anthony Smith, who broke the story of the police chief's request, said of Mr Hurd's dilemma: "If he agrees to sign an order for Hindley's temporary release he could be accused by some MPs of going soft on one of Britain's most evil killers. If he refuses he could be accused of hampering the police inquiry which could take weeks or even months in the desolate landscape without Hindley's on-the-spot help."

What if something went wrong? The security operation would have to be cast-iron. There were those who had sworn to kill her if ever she set foot outside prison walls. Officials were far from happy by the publicity the renewed inquiries had attracted. What about the thousands of sightseers who would certainly flock to the Pennines if the murderess returned to the scene of her crimes? The matter would need many hours, days, perhaps weeks, of serious thought and deliberation.

In the Commons, 200 miles from Saddleworth Moor, there was already a rumbling from MPs, amid suspicions of a 'deal' being made with Myra Hindley. Mr Kenneth Hind, the Tory Member for West Lancashire wanted an assurance from the Home Secretary, particularly for the people of Lancashire, "that should there be evidence to suggest that Miss Myra Hindley is involved in two further murders she will not escape the consequences of her dastardly acts."

Mr Hurd told him: "Immunity from prosecution is a matter for the Attorney General. I understand that in this case he has decided *not* to grant immunity."

Meanwhile, the police activity increased. Police vehicles, the searchers, their dogs, returned to the moors under the determined leadership of Peter Topping, who would follow every lead, every clue, to solve the most challenging case of his, or any other policeman's career.

He had studied the photographs hour after hour, and knew what an enormous task lay ahead. For Saddleworth Moor was not the only place where the camera of Ian Brady had been clicking all those years ago. There were pictures with just the same characteristics, the same postures, as if their subjects had been acting as 'markers', taken 12 miles across the Pennines, in Derbyshire. The spots, in a desolate pine forest, near a twisting, winding road called the Snake Pass, had been pointed out to him by David Smith, insistent that "Brady was too clever to put all his eggs in one basket."

For now, though, Topping was concentrating his efforts and his manpower on Saddleworth Moor. Before them lay miles and miles of barren landscape, with one hillside, valley, ravine, looking much like another and very often lying beneath the grey, swirling mist. He needed Myra Hindley by his side, as soon as possible, before winter hardened the peat and carpeted it with snow.

And he needed to take her back while her mood held, while she still retained her confidence, possibly wavering now the firm 'no deals' pledges were coming from Whitehall and Westminster.

But then came another development that set Myra's mind and pulse racing.

Ian Brady said *he* wanted to help.

IAN BRADY slowly put down the newspaper. So *that* was Myra's game. She had referred to those spots on the moors she had pointed out on the maps as "places that I know were of particular interest *to Ian Brady*." She'd admitted nothing and, it seemed, was trying to pin it all on him. Now she was trying to get back to Saddleworth Moor that had once been *their* place. It seemed she was putting in her two penn'orth because she was scared that he'd beat her to it by confessing everything about them *both*. She thought she was now calling the tune, did she? Well, we'd soon see about that.

He paced the pleasantly furnished room, with its own toilet and colour television set, that had been his home for a year now. What had she been saying to the cops? *About him*? He had been watching the developments on TV, and had been stirred, in a strange, bitter, yet painfully nostalgic way as the cameras had swept the place where he had once walked free with *her*.

Brady smacked his fist into his palm. It looked like she'd be getting *out*. To go *there*. To walk where they had walked when she had loved him.

His mind, with surprising agility for one that had been pronounced sick, travelled back 20 years to when, in their separate worlds of captivity, they had exchanged letters of love that had also referred to their evil complicity. They had written in code to elude censorship, a code they had hastily concocted during their whispered conversations as they had stood trial together in the dock. He had kept all her letters at first, but when she had spurned him for her

71

greater love of liberty he had destroyed them. All but six. His lawyer now had those, safely locked away. They were part of his insurance against the day when she would betray him to further her cause for freedom. That day seemed to be arriving. Had she kept his letters to her? And, if so, how was she using them?

It was time to remind her of *her* letters *he* had kept. And to let Topping know he too was ready to help.

His solicitor, Benedict Birnberg, said next day: "He is very concerned about things that have been said by Myra Hindley implicating him. That has stung him. He wants Myra Hindley and her advisers to know that letters she wrote to him over a period of years when they were first in prison and before their relationship broke up are still in existence." His client, he believed, was now in the mood to talk.

A point to Brady, it seemed, as their bizarre game opened once more. A game, I began to wonder, that in their strange complex minds they were beginning to find a new excitement?

★   ★   ★

COOKHAM Wood women's prison was buzzing with the news. *"Myra's getting out. She's going back on the moors, up North."* Every one of the 120 women serving their sentences in the modern jail knew Prisoner 964055, the woman they called The Queen who, behind the heavy steel cell door had the home comforts of colourful curtains, carpets, plants and pictures on the walls. In surroundings, some bitterly complained, "more like a five-star hotel".

The other prisoners knew that she was now helping the police and that the officers wanted her to join them in their grim search. Myra, surrounded by her 'minders' and the fawning hangers-on, had gained a new respect in the eyes of the sycophants. For she had a way of spellbinding those on both sides of authority. Just as, so long ago, she had won over Lord Longford. But she was not captivating

MPs. One of them, Mr John Ryman, a lawyer and the Labour Member for Blyth Valley wrote to his party leader, Neil Kinnock, urging him to dissociate himself and the party from the views of the Socialist peer.

He wrote: "The nauseating spectacle of a convicted murderess, Myra Hindley, conducting a campaign to ingratiate herself with the police and the Parole Board by tactical confessions has been greatly assisted by the well-meaning, but utterly naive Labour peer Lord Longford. As Lord Longford is a well-known and articulate Labour peer, the public could be forgiven for believing, quite mistakenly, that by implication the Labour Party supports his campaign. Lord Longford does not represent the views of sensible people in the Labour Party. He is a sanctimonious and ridiculous peer who has obviously been hoodwinked by an evil and cold-blooded killer. Lord Longford is guilty of a serious error of judgement in believing that her motives for these revelations are anything other than a calculated, self-interested campaign aimed at currying favour with the Home Office and the Parole Board. In all these circumstances I therefore ask you to emphatically repudiate the views of Lord Longford and make it absolutely clear that he is speaking for himself alone in a personal capacity and not for the Labour Party."

The case was now becoming a political issue and the operation to return Myra Hindley to the Pennines an extremely delicate one. There had still been no official word back from the Home Office, with Douglas Hurd carefully weighing the enormous security risk against the possibility, strongly advocated by Topping, that the murderess could help to pinpoint more graves. Geoffrey Dickens, the Tory MP for Saddleworth in whose constituency the appalling discoveries of two decades ago had been made, was warning: "People round here cannot wait to get their hands on them (Brady and Hindley). I'm convinced they mean business."

He was right. Nowhere was there more hostility towards Myra than Greater Manchester, the place where she was born, grew up, fell in love. And murdered.

Then there were the rumours about other missing people. They could not be children, for there were no other missing youngsters on the police files. But a number of adults had vanished without trace in the area in the 1960s, including a couple of vagrants, whose disappearance from the seamier side of city life would have aroused little curiosity.

Even the cautious Topping was keeping an open mind on "the possibility of other victims". An excitement, a gut feeling that mounts within any good detective, was building up inside the reserved police officer that he was so very close to cracking the murder mystery of the century, a mystery like no other. Not of finding the culprits, they had been under lock and key for a long time, but of finding the victims.

Topping and his men were still on Saddleworth Moor with their dogs, having removed the red flags and white marker tapes to deter the sightseers – the ghouls, as the Press called them – prodding, poking. They needed Myra to point the way, but time was running out.

The first indication was a flicker of his eyelash. Then another as something white, fluffy, instantly melting touched his skin. He looked up at the sky, to a gathering whiteness. The enemy, the first snow of the winter, was falling on Saddleworth Moor.

Chapter Seven

WHERE?

THE snow became a white, whirling frenzy, whipped by an icy east wind that drove it into drifts in the gullies, cloaking whatever secrets they may have hidden, mysteries they might have unravelled. Damn. Topping called in his men, called off the dogs. The animals were useless now, as the Moor became cloaked like an Arctic landscape, masking its features. Only Myra Hindley could help them now.

But there were other investigations to be made, other roads to travel, follow, leading perhaps to other secrets.

Brady and Hindley, she confident, skilful at the wheel of their little car, had travelled far and wide in the ruggedly scenic countryside on Manchester's doorstep, not only into Yorkshire, but into the limestone-rocked county of Derbyshire. Where better, than a place with burning lime in its soil to hide, destroy, bodies? I wondered.

The tormented David Smith had been remembering, as if he could ever forget, the trips that he and his former wife Maureen, Myra's sister, had made with the couple. I spent many hours in the company of Smith while researching *Devil's Disciples*. Now nearing 40, his face etched with the grimness of never being able to put from his mind the nightmare of events of his youth, he has thought often, obsessively, about where the remains of the victims of Ian Brady could be.

Maureen had died from a brain haemorrhage in 1980, seven years after their divorce – the inevitable split that their involvement with the case had caused – and he had remarried, trying with his wife Mary to make a new life for himself, but never being able to escape the old one.

Smith and I travelled in Derbyshire together, he taxing his memory to try to recall exactly where they visited with Brady and Hindley. It had been so long ago and he had always been a back-seat passenger with Brady while the two sisters sat in the front of the Mini.

Smith believed that, as with the excursions to Saddleworth Moor, Brady had deliberately taken them to places that hid awful secrets, that it gave him a strange, evil satisfaction.

One of the places they had visited with the killers was a desolate pine forest near the winding Snake Pass on the Manchester-Sheffield road in the Derbyshire Peak District. He had remembered the dark, eerie place, shadowed by withered pines, that Brady and Myra had chosen for a picnic spot. It was a place where they had been before without the Smiths and where they had taken photographs – with a chilling similarity to the pictures, the pointers to the graves on Saddleworth Moor. Smith had seen the pictures, been through them with the police, in the tartan-backed photograph album that had held the key to unlock the earlier secrets. Two pictures in particular stuck in his mind.

He remembered one of Brady standing about a yard from a rifle resting in the branches of a blackened pine split by lightning. The rifle's barrel was pointing towards the ground, as if focusing on a particular spot. The other showed Myra, lying face down on a blanket, staring fixedly at the ground in the same way as she had stared downwards in that damning photograph that pinpointed the grave of young John Kilbride.

In the 14 months they went out together, the four of them had visited that spot several times, eaten sandwiches, drunk wine. David Smith could not help but wonder if, in darkness, Ian Brady and Myra Hindley had used that barricade of silent pines as a hiding place for two of their secrets of death.

I had persuaded him to repeat the fears he had first voiced 21 years ago to the police, and taken him to the headquarters of Greater Manchester Police to reiterate his suspicions to a new generation of policemen.

Smith had been apprehensive, mindful of the false accusations that Brady and Hindley had made against him, aware too, that the police had paid little attention to his suspicions then, believing that Saddleworth Moor was the *only* graveyard.

He spent two hours with detectives, pouring out every detail he could remember, including those of other places to which he and Maureen had been taken. The officers took down all his recollections, all his suspicions, and put them, like pieces of jigsaw puzzle, into the swelling file of investigation in the hope that they would fit into place in the methodical pattern in which their chief, Topping, was working. Saddleworth was the first priority, for Myra Hindley was saying nothing about other places on the map.

But David Smith had aroused their curiosity and, in the late November of 1986, the detectives took him by car into the Derbyshire countryside, to note and place on file the locations he believed could be of significance.

One place particularly aroused a chilling thought. It was a spot in the hills above the village of Whaley Bridge, 20 miles from Manchester, a place that Smith had mentioned to me when trying to recall the car trips the foursome had taken together. "We stopped at this place, got out and got over a wall and up a very steep climb. Three-quarters of the way up Brady stopped and said 'wait here'. He went on alone, disappearing over the ridge. He must have been gone three-quarters of an hour and when he came back he seemed satisfied, somehow, that everything was as it should be. I couldn't help wondering. I told the police about that too, but they dismissed it. Nobody, they said, would carry a body all that way from the road. But what's wrong with a body *walking* there…?"

This time the police did not dismiss the lonely spot and eventually found and followed the path that Ian Brady had taken.

It led over a ridge to a place that must have provoked a terrible, agonising question, a place that must be left alone for now. A place unquestionably of death.

An old *cemetery*.

77

PETER Topping was keeping an open mind on what horrors his investigations might uncover and on David Smith's assertion that "Ian Brady didn't put all his eggs in one basket." He and his men knew that Saddleworth Moor might not be the only location of graves and that there was a possibility that Brady had claimed victims other than the five youngsters.

One name that has been mentioned often is that of Philip Deare, 20, from Bradford, who had met Brady during his spell in Borstal in the late 1950s. I aired the mystery surrounding his whereabouts in *Devil's Disciples*, pointing out that he had left his home on 21 November 1962 to keep an appointment in Manchester, with Brady, and that detectives in the original investigation had been unable to trace him. I had not been able to find his family while researching *Devil's Disciples* and, while there were claims that he had been a victim of Ian Brady, I could only conclude: "Perhaps he is alive and well somewhere. Perhaps not. The mystery remains."

Now it seems certain that Philip Deare was not, after all, the killer's prey and that he was drowned in an accident in a Sheffield reservoir many years after the Moors Murderers were jailed. Soon after *Devil's Disciples* was published a relative contacted the newspaper I worked for, *The Star*, to tell us of the accident.

But there is still a strange, puzzling aspect to the case of Philip Deare. Myra Hindley knew about the speculation over his fate. She had known of the young man in the early 1960s as a friend of Brady, in the days when her boyfriend had strutted around and talked of robbing banks. In 1985 Brady had talked to Fred Harrison of *The People* newspaper, in hesitant, stilted sentences and was alleged to have said there had been "many more" deaths than those for which he had been jailed, including those of Pauline Reade and Keith Bennett. Asked about Philip Deare he was quoted as saying: "Deare is not connected in any way with the rotten branch that grew out after I met Myra. He was the one who brought getaway cars to us from Manchester."

He drew a veil over questions about what had happened to Deare, refusing to commit himself, save for saying: "It was an accident…I don't know whether the death…" Then silence.

Brady was obviously in an agitated state of mind, parrying, fending off questions and yet being unable, through a remaining, pathetic ego, to strip the aura of mystery with which he had surrounded himself, like a card player, smugly holding the aces. And yet, perhaps, bluffing. The game, as always, being played for the benefit of Myra Hindley.

Twenty-one years earlier detectives had quizzed Brady over Philip Deare. Myra knew that. I discovered, in fact, that the killers referred to him in the coded letters they exchanged between their cells at the remand centre as they awaited trial. The letters, sometimes using riddles, sometimes a system whereby if the first words of each sentence were read vertically, downwards, they spelled out a message, contained a number of chilling exchanges between the murderers.

They included an indication of Brady's venom for David Smith of whom he had said at the trial: "I don't think he is worth hating." But he displayed a different attitude in the hidden message – later deciphered by detectives – in a note to Myra mentioning Smith and her sister thus: "*Smith will die and Maureen, too.*" The communication that most intrigued the policemen was a clumsy pun by Brady… talking of "*our dear friend from Bradford.*"

Although the renewed speculation about Deare two decades later was quoshed by his family, it is doubtful whether Myra Hindley knew of their assertion that he had been drowned. Brady, may have known, may have learned the truth through the prison grapevine, for he *had* referred to "an accident". But, in his twisted, secretive way, had chosen to cloak that knowledge in mystery.

Myra, on the other hand, could have seized on the mystery over Deare to twist it to her own advantage as part of her strategy to get the upper hand in a game that had so far, and for so long been dominated by Ian Brady.

There is no doubt that she was afraid Brady was on the verge of a full confession and she wanted to get her story in first, told to her own advantage, before he had chance to incriminate her.

Myra Hindley had the power to dominate, manipulate other prisoners ever since her days in Holloway and, cunningly, would feed to those about to be released information she wanted to be known to the world outside. On Sunday, 23 November 1986 – exactly 23 years after young John Kilbride met his death – the huge headline in *The People* was the result of her scheming. MYRA NAMES BRADY'S SECRET VICTIM.

The message came from Rena Duffy, recently released from Cookham Wood, saying that Myra was not living the life of luxury that others imagined, that she was subjected to taunts and jibes, making her life hell. She always slept with her light on, "because her mind is so tortured."

And then the allegation, made by the murderess in a whispered conversation. "Myra knows Brady killed Deare", Rena Duffy was quoted as saying. "She's kept the details to herself as an insurance against Brady shopping her for more crimes. But now I think she's ready to tell. She never told me how or where but she left me in no doubt that she knows."

So, Myra was pointing the finger at Brady for the murder of Philip Deare. But if the young man *was* accidentally drowned so recently, then she had been caught out in a deliberate lie to frame him.

SHE felt a strange, chilling sensation about the prospect of returning, after all that time, to Saddleworth Moor. There was a mounting excitement, heightened by a gnawing fear. For while the walls of jail had imprisoned her for more than 20 years, they had also shielded her from those who wanted to kill her, and she knew that if she went back to the Pennines they would certainly try.

The excitement was that of a woman who had taken life

or death chances in that place of evil before. For remember that while Myra Hindley and Ian Brady had been murdering and burying the terrible evidence of their frightful crimes, the death penalty was still in force. They were still hanging people for murder. The last two men to go to the scaffold in Britain, Peter Anthony Allen and Glynne Owen Evans, who murdered a laundry van driver, were executed on 13 August 1964, more than a year after Pauline Reade vanished, nine months after John Kilbride met his death and four months before Lesley Ann Downey was taken to share their burial ground.

That had been the added spice to the cruel game played by Brady and Hindley in the 1960s. The risk and the consequences of getting caught. Just before her arrest, Myra had scarcely been able to contain her excitement after David Smith had witnessed the brutal murder of Edward Evans. As the three of them sat in her council house living room, the body of their teenage victim callously trussed up in a bedroom upstairs, his life's blood oozing from 14 axe wounds in his head, she had asked Brady if he remembered when they were nearly caught. She had been sitting on the moors in the Mini-van while he was getting ready to dispose of a body. "Do you remember the time we were on the moors and we had a body in the back? The time a policeman came up?"

Her voice had risen. "You were over the hill digging a grave and a police car came up and asked me what the trouble was." She had told the policeman her spark plugs were wet and she was drying them off.

"And all the time I was praying that you didn't come over the top of the hill."

Myra Hindley had not felt a raw chill like that since the day that Mr Justice Fenton Atkinson, six months after the abolition of capital punishment, had said when jailing them for life: "I pass the only sentence which the law *now* allows."

Now they were considering letting her go back to where she had so wantonly mis-spent her youth, thrown away her liberty. And yet a place of such inexplicable painful nostalgia. A place of death. To seek death and where death might come looking for her.

Outwardly she maintained an air of calmness, almost serenity, an attitude to tell everyone: "Look what a good girl I'm being." Her solicitor told the world she was still prepared to help the police, no matter what the consequences, or whatever Ian Brady might think, say or do. And she was not frightened of his threats about the letters she had sent to him.

For someone whose every day for 20 years had been the same, as predictable as the one before, the looming probability that she would return to Saddleworth filled Myra's every waking thought with an anticipation, maybe a thrill of facing the unknown. Perhaps an adventure.

Meanwhile, in Manchester, the anger of the families of her victims was rising at it always did when their suspicions of her motives were aroused. The father of John Kilbride was particularly incensed. Patrick Kilbride, now 58, felt the hatred return for the woman he blamed for the destruction of his life. He and his wife Sheila, a quiet, gentle woman, were divorced five years after their son's disappearance. She had once told me that she disliked his strictness with their children. For Irish-born Patrick had a quick temper, more easily inflamed after the dreadful way in which they had lost the eldest of their seven children.

He now lived in Oldham, the neighbouring town to Ashton-under-Lyne, on whose market ground John was last seen alive 23 years earlier. Alone with his thoughts he vowed to himself that if either of the Moors Murderers was allowed to return to the scene of their crimes he would do everything possible to get at them. "I'm not bothered about what happens to me, or if I get sent down." He shrugged. "That's the least of my worries because they have ruined my life anyway."

Sheila, living in her little flat in Ashton, begged her four sons not to try to take the law into their own hands. Now 54, Sheila told me: "I've told my lads to leave Myra Hindley alone if she comes back. She could do some good for once by helping to end the agony of other mothers." A tear crept down her cheek with the memory of her son's fate as she whispered: "I really believe the police will find something up there. I've always believed it."

Her eldest son Danny, now 33, who had shared a bedroom with the big brother he still painfully misses and once had a warning visit from Scotland Yard officers after publicly threatening to kill Myra Hindley agreed with his violence-hating mother this time. He nodded as we chatted at his home two miles from Sheila's, where he lives with his wife Anne and four children. "I know I've said I'll do her in if I get the chance. But it won't be *this* time. Not this time. Now she has a job to do." It grated to think of *her* practically walking on what had been his brother's grave, but, said Danny: "I've also told my brothers to stay away. They're very angry and one of them has talked about going up there with a gun. But I won't let him." He knew, though, that dissuading his father would be far, far more difficult.

And Ian Brady was feeling the whiplash of the renewed publicity over his crimes. Once more he found himself placed in isolation, the solitary confinement in which he had spent most of his prison life for self-protection. Other mental patients it was said had threatened to kill him.

THERE had been no real escape from the anger for Ian Brady and Myra Hindley. Contempt, loathing and, often, violence, had never been far away. From his earliest days in prison, Brady had exercised his rights under Rule 43 of the prison regulations and had spent much of his sentence in solitary confinement. His rare contact with other inmates had been mainly with those of his own ilk, other child killers and molesters.

Myra, on the other hand, while loathing her incarceration, had through her cleverness and guile, led a freer, less frightened life in jail. Of course there had been attacks, some of them vicious – like the time in Holloway when her nose had been broken – and she still had to be careful not to turn her back on some. But she had had the cunning knack, the art of survival, in knowing to whom to show her hard side and to whom to display her soft side – though that side, say many, was counterfeit.

She had used her body to wheedle her way into the company of the toughest women in jail, the dykes, the lesbians and had been one of them for many years since first realising how easy it had been to manipulate others through bestowing sexual favours. In Holloway she had formed a relationship with prison officer Patricia Cairns, a former Carmelite nun who was so smitten by her that she even tried to help her to escape. The plan failed and Cairns paid the penalty with a six-year jail sentence.

Myra surrounded herself with 'toughies' who acted as minders to protect her from women sickened by her crimes and by the privileges she enjoyed.

She had another form of protection, another way to buy favours. For she was so well connected that she was able to get her hands on a valuable currency – cannabis. It was a secret revealed by one of her former minders Terri Nankivill, a strapping five foot ten inch redhead who had kept her eye on the murderess for seven months, along with two coloured girls. "She's always got dope to sell for favours or protection and she never puts her hand in her purse like the other girls," said Terri after her release.

The softer side of Myra, the side she showed to the public, the side she showed to Topping, was still saying she was ready, determined, to help to end the suffering of Joan Reade and Winnie Johnson, even though, said her lawyer, she was in 'a rather frail' condition. And Topping was just as determined to do all he could to get her back on the moors.

He had already held long talks with the Home Office Prison Department, whose main concern was still the security aspect of taking such a bold, controversial step. How could they avoid the publicity? Officials even talked about the possibility of appealing to editors for a news blackout – a system used frequently in kidnapping cases. And for only a small, picked contingent of journalists to be allowed to report the event – just as a royal visit was conducted.

Ian Brady, meanwhile, was being more cagey, while wanting to keep the upper hand over Myra. Yes, he was prepared to meet the police, under certain conditions. He wanted his lawyer to be there and, "I want a guarantee of no recordings. No tapes." He was only too painfully aware that a tape recording, so long ago, had helped to trap him.

He had studied the newspapers, listened to the radio, watched television. "It's a bloody media circus." But still he wanted to get in on the act. In fact, be top of the bill.

And so, on Tuesday, 25 November 1986, Detective Chief Superintendent Peter Topping found himself in Newman Ward of the Park Lane Special Hospital in Liverpool, facing Ian Stewart Brady.

Ready to talk, for the first time in 21 years, one month and 18 days, about the Moors Murders.

Chapter Eight

A MACABRE JOKE?

THE two men were of similar age. They had both been little boys during the War, had heard the air raid sirens warning of Hitler's bombs, had gone to school in an age of ration books and clothing coupons. They had probably whistled and hummed the same Johnny Ray and Frankie Laine songs in the Teddy Boy era of their teens. And they had both turned to crime as a way of life when they were young men. It was at that point that their lives took vastly different paths. For the middle-aged men now facing each other were Peter Topping, policeman, and Ian Brady, multiple murderer.

Their eyes searched each others faces: Brady's, the sunken cheeks now filling out a little, pale from more than 21 years of imprisonment; Topping's whipped pink by the wind while investigating those deeds 50 miles from the secure hospital where they now sat, patient and visitor, with murder on their minds.

It had been almost a year and a half since their first, and last, meeting, when Brady had been in Gartree and had clasped his plastic hot water bottle to his stomach with his bony hands. And said nothing when Topping had asked him about Pauline Reade and Keith Bennett. This time, though, there was a different, perhaps calmer, air about Ian Brady who had, surprisingly, agreed to see the police chief there and then.

Topping had gone to Park Lane with Detective Inspector Geoff Knupfer to meet hospital officials and Brady's solicitor, to pave the way for his hoped-for confrontation with the killer. They chatted for almost an hour with Benedict Birnberg who, unexpectedly, told them: "He'll see you today." The detective was shown into another room where Britain's most infamous murderer was waiting.

It was a pulsating moment, one that neither would ever forget, as they faced each other in that room. Topping took in Brady's gaunt appearance, the cold grey eyes, the hair, now sprinkled with grey, but still quiffed in the style he had chosen as a young man when everybody was copying Tony Curtis. The mouth was small, still cruel.

The CID man cleared his throat and exchanged a greeting with Brady, whose hard, flat Glaswegian tones had remained unsoftened by more than 30 years in England.

Topping, as was his way, was polite, patient as, with the solicitor sitting alongside them, he slowly, quietly, in a manner to coax and not antagonise or silence his quarry, talked of his investigation in a mode so unofficial, casual, that he might have been discussing the weather. He had to try to win the man's confidence, not remind him of those voices in his head... *"We are making inquiries about the whereabouts of..."*

Their voices were a drone in the corridor of a hospital that went about its business while the reporters, the photographers, waited outside the gates in the November drizzle. What was Brady telling Topping?

Whatever it had been, Topping was not saying when, two hours later, he emerged from the building. "The contents of the interview are confidential. I would like to see him again though no arrangements have been made." He was sorry, but that was it. Nothing more to say. And the policeman took whatever secrets Ian Brady may have imparted back to his office in Greater Manchester police headquarters.

The search, meanwhile, was continuing on Saddleworth Moor as the snow gave way to rain, turning the peat to a quagmire, soft, oozing, but still unyielding. And, mockingly providing the officers and their panting dogs with the false alarm of scraps of tattered cloth that turned out to be nothing of significance when the forensic scientists examined them. But it meant an all-night search under floodlights in case other clues became washed away or buried beneath one of the frequent snowstorms on the Moor.

There was, by now, a tremendous Press presence, just as there had been 21 years ago. Every room in the little hotels and inns of the villages in the valley below was taken. And caravans, hired by newspapers so their men could keep a round-the-clock vigil were dotting the landscape outside the search perimeter, on tracks and in Crowther's farmyard. The target of the lensmen was Myra Hindley. Their editors had been told by their parliamentary lobby correspondents that Douglas Hurd would say "Yes" and that the murderess could be taken back to Saddleworth at any time.

RAF spotter planes were flying over the area, as they had in 1965, looking for minute, but tell-tale signs in the landscape that could yield clues for the searchers.

The weather was now getting worse with snow, sleet, hail, rain and a bitterly cold wind reminding Topping that time, for 1986, had almost run out. Once the Pennines were gripped by the worst of winter he would have to call off the search for months.

And, for the first time, the detective was now facing criticism.

THE criticism came from Geoffrey Dickens, the Conservative MP for Saddleworth, a man who had crusaded fiercely against the evils of child abuse and for the restoration of capital punishment for the killers of children. His intention now, he said, was to spare the relatives of the victims of Brady and Hindley from distress, complaining that the search of the Moor was upsetting them. "It would be an act of mercy if the police end their search soon and not continue next spring", he said.

It was a brickbat that dismayed the CID chief, a direct contradiction of his heartfelt intention: to try to bring comfort to those families. Topping blinked through the rain at the pressmen who had relayed the criticism. "That is certainly not the attitude they have reflected to me", he said carefully.

"I am, however, very concerned about them and I can quite understand that this sort of activity and publicity could cause them considerable distress. I will be seeing them – and their views *are* important and *will* be taken into account – but they have suffered 20 or more years of great anguish already. It would appear that the one way they see of putting that to rest would be to be able to bury their children in a proper grave and have their remains treated with just respect."

Topping, who, like Doug Nimmo so many years before, had been deeply affected by the sadness of the parents of Pauline Reade and Keith Bennett was hurt and angered as the barbs continued to fly his way. Worse, there was talk that he had fallen for a ploy by the Moors Murderess who was trying to regain her freedom. No, said Topping firmly, he was *not* being misled by Myra Hindley. Her information had merely confirmed conclusions he and his men had reached already.

Topping went back to the families, to Winnie Johnson and to Amos Reade, whose wife was now in hospital, unable to bear the dreadful strain that the revived activity had caused. Winnie Johnson had cried and told him her only desire in life now was for her son's body to be found and to be able to give him a proper burial. Amos Reade had nodded. Yes, go on with the search.

Yes, Topping told the pressmen. The search *would* go on. "I owe it to the families of the missing children." Was he aware of what was being said? The detective's eyes glinted. "I am aware," he said slowly, "that in this part of the world there is still a great deal of concern that two children went missing and no-one has discovered what actually happened to them."

Myra Hindley was aware of the mounting criticism, too, that people were saying the police were on a wild goose chase.

It was time to bring Winnie Johnson back into the game.

MRS JOHNSON was shocked and then puzzled when the news was passed on to her. *Myra Hindley wanted to see her.*

She wanted the mother, plagued with grief and uncertainty, to visit her in prison, even pay her fare for the long journey from Manchester to Kent. Mrs Johnson shook her head. What *was* her motive? *Why* did she want to talk to her? The thought of coming face to face with the murderess was frightening and yet, if she could summon the courage, tempting. What *was* Hindley up to?

Myra had made the strange suggestion in a letter to the Reverend Peter Timms, a Methodist minister and former prison governor who had been visiting her in Cookham Wood. "I'm sorry to have to write to you in such an urgent manner when I should have written to you a long time ago," she told him. "Because of the nature of this present matter I know you will understand if I save my explanations for my ever-long silence."

Then she referred to Mrs Johnson's letter which she had said had been the catalyst that had broken her silence. "I'm enclosing a copy of a letter I received on Friday October 31. It is a heartbreaking letter as you will see when you read it. Mrs Johnson is heartbroken and when I read it in the Deputy Governor's office it broke my heart. No words can express what I feel for that poor desperate woman. And I am desperate. I desperately want to write to her myself. I want to send her the money so she can come and visit me, so I can talk to her. But for obvious reasons I can do neither. For I know that the Press will find out and use and abuse Mrs Johnson and myself."

The clergyman spoke of the letter on TV. On Channel 4's *Seven Days* programme he said: "I believe she is penitent. She is truly sorry and this letter to me is one of the indicators of that." He was convinced her feelings were genuine.

Winnie Johnson did make that 250-mile journey to Cookham Wood Prison, taken there not at Myra's expense, but by *The Sun* newspaper. She was clinging to the hope that perhaps there was some truth in the words of the obviously convinced Mr Timms and that the killer really did feel the pity and remorse she had expressed. Perhaps, some way, she could jog her memory by reminding her of that night, that date, 16 June 1964 and of the short-sighted little lad who had disappeared from the face of the earth. And Mrs Johnson knew, had walked straight into hell.

But Winnie Johnson's journey was in vain. She had had a letter passed to Myra, telling her she was waiting…"in the hope that you will not prolong my agony." The reply came via Mr Fisher, Myra's solicitor, who said she had told him that such a meeting would be "enormously distressing."

The mother returned to Manchester in tears.

THE nightmare went on, too, for Margaret Brady and Nellie Moulton, the mothers who had borne children whose names, once lovingly given, were now almost always prefixed with the word evil. Evil Ian Brady. Evil Myra Hindley. There is no doubt that the long-ago union of their son and daughter had destroyed their lives. They could not blot the existence of them from their minds. And painfully, heartbreakingly, they could not stop loving them.

Neither, even after 21 years, could they stop asking themselves, in countless anguished moments, *Why?* Why did they do it?

Mrs Brady had been to see her son only once since his transfer to Park Lane a year ago. She had visited him on his birthday, 2 January, and had tea with the man she had first held in her arms 48 years ago and whom they now called a monster. She knew he had felt uncomfortable, even embarrassed by her being there and by the watching attendants, self-conscious, too, of his emaciated appearance. She had stayed away, but they had kept in touch by letter.

Her son was obviously now in a better physical

condition than when she had last seen him. He had put on weight – his body had wasted to a frail eight stones in prison – and he was more communicative to those around him. When he had first been transferred to the mental hospital he had been withdrawn, shunning other patients, seeking the isolation he had had in jail.

His quarters had been in the geriatric ward, away from the younger inmates, some of whom had threatened him.

Now, though, he seemed to have a new sense of purpose, of importance. For the first time, perhaps, since the police had arrested him demeaningly, perhaps comically in other circumstances, in only his vest he was beginning to feel the big shot he once thought he was.

Margaret Brady, now 76 – her husband Patrick, who gave his name to his stepson, to be blackened forever, collapsed and died in the street at the age of 48 soon after the trial – had borne the shame with dignity, keeping herself to herself in her little Manchester flat. She still could not understand what had possessed her son, her flesh and blood, to do what he did to those children. She did not make excuses for him, only shook her head sadly with the recollection that – as far as she knew – he had done nothing really *bad* until he met Myra Hindley. Mothers often blame the misdeeds of their children upon falling into bad company. Margaret Brady was no exception.

Across the city, in another little council flat, living still, bravely, in the same area, Gorton, where her daughter and Ian Brady began their wicked liaison and where Pauline Reade took her last walk to her death, Nellie Moulton had endured the same pain.

She feared answering the door, expecting every knock to be that of a reporter, leaving her second husband Bill, a lorry driver, to deal with unknown and unwelcome callers when he was at home. The attention, the whole business, Mr Moulton would tell the visitors, was killing Nellie.

Margaret Brady and Nellie Moulton had shared the life sentences of their son and their daughter.

Mrs Brady, alone with her many thoughts, painfully exacerbated by the recent events, was also wary of callers.

So it was with the usual defensive caution that she answered her front door bell on the evening of Sunday 30 November. She peered through the darkness at the woman, blonde, middle-aged, standing on the step. It was someone she had never expected to see, though she was often in her thoughts. And when her visitor introduced herself the grey-haired Scots lady could scarcely believe her ears. She was seized with apprehension, yet great pity. Her caller was another mother, someone else serving a life sentence for what Ian and Myra had done.

Ann West.

THE two mothers looked at each other in the shaft of electric light that cut the cold haze of the night air outside the front porch. There was no anger or hate in Ann West's eyes, voice, or her heart, as, with Alan beside her, she gently asked the old lady if she would talk to her. Mrs Brady, the questions forming in her mind – she had heard of the rage of Ann West – nevertheless opened the door wider. "Come in," she said softly and the younger woman and her husband followed her into the comfortable little living room.

The visit had not been easy for Mrs West, but she had been driven to make it by the relentless force that had fuelled her detest of Myra Hindley's long battle for liberty. "Oh yes," she had told me, "I hate Ian Brady, but I hate her even more. Now, it seemed, Ian Brady was on the verge of cooperating with the police. And he, who did not want to be free, had nothing to gain. Or lose. Could his mother get through to him where others had failed?

Apart from that, Mrs West had something to say to the mother of her daughter's murderer that had been in her heart for a long, long time. That she bore no malice to Margaret Brady, that she could not be blamed for the sins of her son.

Mrs Brady, gladdened, warmed by the words, shook her head. She wanted Ian to tell the truth. Why had he – and

Myra Hindley – waited so long? Why had they prolonged it all by their silence? But she couldn't disown her Ian, despite his wickedness. "You've no idea what I've been through," she said. "I can't imagine what its been like for you and the other parents."

The two mothers talked for almost three hours finding strange comfort in talking openly about the subject that had dwarfed everything else for them. They were glad they had met.

THE Home Office had still not announced its decision over whether or not to allow Myra to return to the scene of her crimes. Once again, Peter Topping, with his men still on the bitterly-cold moors, was in Whitehall, talking for more than four hours to officials about the security aspects, telling them why he attached such great importance to her going back to Saddleworth.

The next day, in anorak and woollen hat, he rejoined his team and with the wind buffeting his words outside the mobile caravan headquarters that had been set up on the borders of Greater Manchester and West Yorkshire he reiterated his determination to go on searching – with or without the company of Myra Hindley. There was a lot of talking to do at the Home Office but, he said: "The search is something I want to complete."

By then the search area – close to the trail of the Pennine Way, trekked by thousands of hikers travelling the Backbone of England over the years – had spread hundreds of yards from the area where the bodies of Lesley Ann Downey and John Kilbride had been found. But all that had been found so far in the vast acreage were scraps of material that had been eliminated as having no connection with the inquiry and the bleached bones of sheep.

The next day, Topping was again heading south, this time to Cookham Wood for a two-and-a-half hour talk with Myra, amid a growing, cynical belief that he was on a wild goose chase.

The *Daily Express* reported that Home Secretary Hurd was "angry at the publicity surrounding the hunt – believing police have only succeeded in helping Hindley in an attempt to put over a compassionate image to help her campaign for release." It was the police chief's fourth visit to the murderess's cell and when he left, her solicitor, who had been there while Topping talked to her, said she was "very tired and exhausted."

In fact, the so-far strong-willed Myra Hindley was beginning to show the signs of strain. The publicity had, indeed, been intense. And most of it adverse. She was *still* Evil Myra to the press, in spite of leaked suggestions that she intended to tell the Parole Board not to consider her case when it was next reviewed in four years' time. She was unable to sleep and was refusing to take exercise because of the battery of cameras poised for a glimpse as the newsmen camped outside the jail. She did only inside work now, like decorating the prison kitchen. Like Ian Brady she had sought solitude.

She was thinner and looked older, even being described by one prison officer as "a wizened old lady" who saw her chances of freedom slipping away." She sees herself as some kind of heroine, but she takes a lot of stick from the staff and other inmates. They tease her about Christmas being so close and that there are only a few more shopping days left. You wouldn't recognise her now," said the officer. "She has changed so much since the last pictures were taken of her. She has all but given up on any hopes of parole. She feels the recent publicity about the new search has killed off all possibility and this has hit her hard."

The search, meanwhile, in biting wind and driving rain, was now being carried out on the West Yorkshire side of the boundary, a mile from the original spot, crying out for a guide. Mr Fisher was saying that Myra had not had second thoughts about going to the Moor, though "she would obviously prefer not to have to do this. She is willing to go up there if the police feel it is necessary and the Home Office allow it."

Yet again, on Friday 12 December, Topping made the

journey south to Cookham Wood Prison. *Was* Myra cracking up? Or was she shamming? The critics were again closing in. His Chief Constable, James Anderton was to be questioned by the Greater Manchester Police Authority about how much it was all costing. And Mr Geoffrey Dickens had forwarded a letter he had received to the Home Secretary.

The anonymous letter, purporting to come from a woman prison officer at Cookham Wood, had said: "I am writing to express deep concern that the establishment and the public do not become taken in by Hindley's sudden desire to be of so-called assistance with regard to the finding of the bodies on the Saddleworth Moors. She is looking upon it all as a macabre joke...never has she shown any remorse for her evil deeds. She is totally without conscience or guilt. The only thing she feels is the desire to be released – in other words she is stir crazy. She has only spoken out now to get her word in before Brady – she has told me so – as she is scared he will reveal even more atrocities she was responsible jointly with him for.

"Hindley is a menace to society and should suffer the ultimate penalty for her unmitigated evil. There is no redeeming feature in the creature that she is. It is an insult to womankind to call her a woman. Brady may be called mad, but at least he does know better than to want to be free. Please God do not let Hindley be free – there is enough evil in the world already."

Mr Dickens wanted the Home Secretary to consider the letter before deciding on Myra's temporary release, but Mr Hurd had already decided. And though he remained silent, stone-faced when he left, Topping had spent two hours at Cookham Wood finalising the arrangements.

The plans had been made, the stage had been set, for Myra Hindley to return to Saddleworth Moor in four days' time.

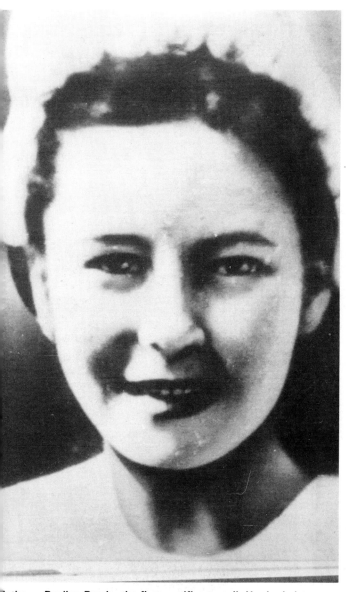

Victim.....Pauline Reade, the first sacrifice to evil. Her body lay on Saddleworth Moor for 24 years.

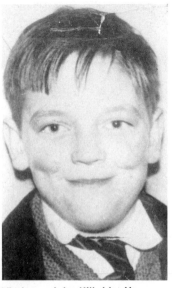

Victim.....John Kilbride. He was lured away from the market ground at Ashton-under-Lyne.

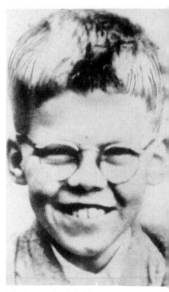

Victim.....Keith Bennett, vanished in 1964. He is still missing.

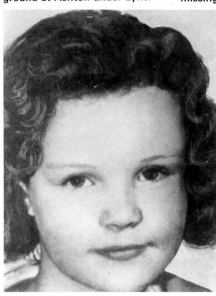

Victim.....Lesley Ann Downey. Her tape-recorded voice damned Brady and Hindley.

The policeman who never gave up, despite fierce criticism. Detective Chief Superintendent Peter Topping spent day after day, week after week, often on his hands and knees in the black peat....until it finally yielded one of its grim secrets.

In Keith's footsteps....Mrs Winifred Johnson, with Detective Chief Superintendent Peter Topping, on the Moor where her young son's life ended in the summer of 1964.

An aerial view of Saddleworth Moor showing the areas, taped off by police, where the search for bodies was resumed in 1986.

Ian Brady visits the Moors in July 1987, and points out a possible grave to Peter Topping.

The avenging father, Patrick Kilbride with the knife with which he stalked Myra Hindley when she returned to Saddleworth Moor.

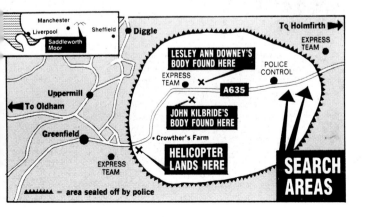

Manchester
Liverpool
Sheffield
Saddleworth Moor

Diggle
To Holmfirth ➡

EXPRESS TEAM

LESLEY ANN DOWNEY'S BODY FOUND HERE

POLICE CONTROL

EXPRESS TEAM
✕
A635

Uppermill

✕
JOHN KILBRIDE'S BODY FOUND HERE

To Oldham ⬅

Greenfield
• Crowther's Farm

HELICOPTER LANDS HERE
✕

EXPRESS TEAM

SEARCH AREAS

〰️〰️〰️ = area sealed off by police

Victim.....Edward Evans, the murderers' final sacrifice.

Flashback to 1965. The original search for the victims of the Moors Murderers. Five police forces - Cheshire, Lancashire, Manchester, Derbyshire and West Riding of Yorkshire - were involved. The long probing rods they used were replaced by new techniques 21 years later....and a team of just nine men.

The grave. Police search for further clues at the spot covered by a white tent, where the body of Pauline Reade was found.

Haunted. David Smith, the former brother-in-law of Myra Hindley, cursed by the killers after his evidence brought them to justice, returns to Saddleworth Moor.

The house of horror. Number 16 Wardle Brook Avenue in 1965....and just before its demolition 22 years later.

Chapter Nine

RETURN TO HELL

For the lips of strange woman drop as an honeycomb, and her mouth is smoother than oil:
But her end is bitter as wormwood, sharp as a two-edged sword.
Her feet go down to death; her steps take hold on hell.

PROVERBS, 5:3.

ONE by one, like candles being lit, like the flaps on an advent card being opened, the lights were going on in the houses and cottages in the little villages of the valley as dawn crept over the ridge of The Moor above them. Mothers would soon be calling to their children, warm and safe, to get up for school.

It was nine days from Christmas. The decorations sparkled, the letters to Santa Claus had been written, and the cotton wool snowflakes stuck on the insides of the windows might now be unnecessary as the real thing, soft but icy cold, began to flutter from the heavens.

The villagers of Greenfield, Uppermill, Diggle, Delph and Dobcross rubbed the sleep from their eyes. Fathers, cursing the cold and the sleet, stomped out for work. Mothers gently shook their sons and daughters. "Come on now, you'll be late. Only a few days to go. And aren't you one of The Wise Men, or Mary, in the Nativity play? Paul, Tracey. Come on, now. I shan't tell you again."

The kids grumbled sleepily, but left their warm, cosy beds, to be cheered as they looked outside by the promise of a white Christmas. They'd be late if they didn't hurry, warned the mums, some of them leaving now for their office desks, their shop counters, their mill sewing machines. "Now think on. Straight home tonight."

How smashing Christmas was, thought the youngsters as, with the mantelpiece clocks creeping towards nine o'clock, and fuelled with Weetabix and Rice Krispies, they turned the silent streets leading to school into a whooping melee, the thin layer of slush melting disappointingly in their reddened hands before it could be transformed into mischievously intended snowballs.

High above them as they filed, pink-cheeked, to their desks, a few short miles but a world, a heaven, a hell apart from the classrooms with their pictures of Baby Jesus and Mary and Joseph on the walls, the wind was harsher, the showers heavier. But the moan of the wind was for once outdone by a drone, becoming louder, clattering now, its blades sending the sleet horizontally. A man-made machine, a helicopter, slowing, descending, then hovering before slowly coming to rest in a place where one of its passengers had been before, many years ago, in a Mini.

Straight home tonight, the mothers in the valley had said, just as mothers all over Britain had warned their children, echoing the words of their own mothers 20-odd years ago when kids had gone missing. One of the reasons for the caution had been the deeds, then undetected, of that passenger, a woman.

Myra Hindley had returned to Saddleworth Moor.

WITH a clang that shattered the silence of the dark early hours, the lock had been drawn back on the heavy steel cell door, a shaft of light from the bulb in the corridor outside penetrating the gloom, revealing dimly the pale face of the woman on the bed.

But Prisoner 964055 was already awake, sleep impossible as with a child on Christmas morning or as with the condemned on the eve and day of his, or her, execution.

Silenty she rose from the bed and sank slowly to her knees before the crucifix on the wall of the room, ten feet long by seven feet wide, where she had schemed, planned for her freedom, for this chance to go back to the world, albeit one of evil, that she had known as a young woman. Now, that cell, those walls that she had cursed for imprisoning her, suddenly seemed so safe. She felt a chilling, creeping dread and her prayers became more fervent, urgent, demanding, then pleading. Please God, keep her safe. Myra Hindley was afraid.

Now she almost wished that, like in the films when someone was about to go to the scaffold, the prison governor would appear and say she had been reprieved, that she didn't have to go after all. For in Myra's mind that fateful day, 16 December 1986, the excitement, the anticipation of adventure that she had first felt at the prospect of going back to those brooding Pennines, was being replaced by a growing unease.

And a sickening dismay with the knowledge that if they did let her go completely she would never *really* be free. She had cheated the hangman, but out there she would always have to look over her shoulder for those who had sworn to step into his shoes as executioner. Stop it Myra, she chided herself for her doubts, her fears and dressed slowly.

She couldn't eat breakfast and sipped at the hot tea that had been brought to her cell. Would, *could* someone try to kill her? She could do with something a bit stronger than this tea, like that German wine that had once bolstered her guts. She could barely remember its taste now.

There were voices outside – the two women prison officers who would be going with her. Then more footsteps, voices, in the corridor – policemen coming to get her. Don't worry. She'd be safe enough. Everything had been taken care of. *Ready*?

Myra rose, glanced once more around her cell, at the pictures of her mam and Sharon, her niece, Maureen's little girl by her second marriage. Poor Maureen. Another long look at the crucifix, please, God. And she followed the detectives down the corridor, past the other cells where the girls were waking up and the whisper was going around. "She's on her way..."

She probably envied them in a way, safely locked up. Such was the irony of Myra Hindley's impending taste of freedom.

Through the governor's office and outside, the cold morning air, the blackness of night beginning to give way to the grey light of dawn, sent a reminiscent shiver through her body. She pulled the black scarf over her face until only her eyes were showing. It had been a long, long time since she was outside at this time of the morning.

A police car, a Granada, was waiting, its engine purring, the pale blue smoke from its exhaust spluttering in the wind. One of the detectives opened the back door and she ducked inside to the pleasant warmth and that 'new car' smell she had loved when she bought her Mini.

The doors slammed shut and the car moved off, its wheels crunching on the gravel drive, then out, through the big double gates, 18 feet high, that had held her captive, but kept her safe. There was a police car in front of them, another one closed up behind. C-registered. Her Mini-Traveller had been a 'C', CNC 153C, except the Cs now prefixed the registration numbers. God, they'd been right through the alphabet while she'd been inside.

The cars picked up speed, past the Pressmen who had kept an all-night vigil and were now dialling the numbers of their news editors on their mobile telephones. "*She's on her way.*" The small convoy turned onto the main road just outside Rochester, the A229 with its signposts illuminated by the headlights including, oddly, creepily significant for the occasion, *Gravesend*. The Kent countryside slipped by, past signs for places like Capstone, Walderslade and Blue Bell Hill. The eyes above the black scarf watching the hedges flying by took it all in greedily, feasting themselves on the world.

They reached the motorway, the M20, heading towards London, but only went as far as junction 4 to the A228 and West Malling airfield, and her transport, a Metropolitan Police helicopter, waiting to take her to the next road, this time one she had known very well, 250 miles away. The A635 over Saddleworth Moor.

★   ★   ★

THE helicopter roared into life. Slowly the blades began to turn, then faster. The noise grew. As the machine rose from the ground Myra clenched her fists with the nervous excitement that comes with a first flight. The airfield buildings below them grew smaller as they gained height and droned in a north-westerly direction, up the country towards Manchester. It was the quickest and, more importantly, the safest way for her to travel.

Her visit now was no secret and ahead of her lay an amazing security operation. The police were leaving nothing to chance. And Saddleworth Moor was being turned into a fortress.

It was 4.30am, still dark, when a convoy of ten police vehicles wound its way up the A635 in a snowstorm, the snowflakes growing bigger as it climbed. There were seven Ford Transit vans, two dog vans and a Land Rover. The vehicles' passengers were members of the Tactical Aid Group. And they were armed.

Roadblocks were set up, one at the west end of the road near Greenfield, and another in the east towards the little Yorkshire town of Holmfirth. The job of the armed men was to patrol the miles of moorland, now whitening – and providing a background to make a target stand out more easily – to prevent anyone getting anywhere near a rifle sight's distance of 'The Visitor'.

More police cars, vans, Range Rovers, began to arrive, converging on a quarry lay-by where the mobile incident room, the operational base was stationed on the Yorkshire side of the boundary on the narrow road to the village of Meltham.

Two reporters and six photographers had spent a cold, uncomfortable night on the freezing Moor, sitting in their cars in another lay-by on the plateau at the summit. A police Transit van pulled up alongside. They'd have to

101

move. The Pressmen pleaded, protested, argued, promised to do anything the police asked if they could stay. Well, said the officer in charge, staying where they were would mean just that. They wouldn't be able to move from that spot all day. Not for anything. The newsmen nodded in agreement, thankful for the nearby ditch, out of sight of the road, for when nature called.

Then more officers arrived on the Moor, this time in a 54-seater Greater Manchester Police coach, its path through the thickening snow on the road laid by a gritting lorry. The policemen, the Pressman, looked up at the sky and the swirling whiteness, now developing into a blizzard. Surely they'd never bring her in this. But the operation went on. Orders were briskly issued. "Go and search those Pressmen and their cars. Give them identification cards." The reporters and photographers were grimly warned: "Go on that Moor and you'll get lifted. Understood?"

There was an edginess about the policemen, caught up by the tension of the occasion. The first of the cars were turned away at the checkpoint road blocks, their drivers puzzled. Scores of journalists stood in the sleet outside the darkened, locked and bolted Clarence pub in Greenfield, wondering what was going on up there, just a few miles away.

The armed policemen checked their .762 calibre sniper's rifles and looked towards the skyline. Visibility was now down to less than 50 yards, though the snow had thinned to a freezing drizzle. Then they heard it. Softly at first then louder, a noise like the beating of wings of a huge bird of prey, breaking the quietness of Saddleworth Moor. It came down, through the mist, its white and red paint bright against the stark background, pausing, hovering a few feet from the ground, the wind from its blades flattening the coarse brown grass, its noise drowning the voices of the waiting policemen.

A few seconds later, the Metropolitan Police helicopter touched down on the A635 just as, a world away in the valley below, the shopkeepers were unbolting their front doors and the last young stragglers were panting up the school yards. Myra Hindley had come back to hell.

And already someone, a father, was stalking her with a knife.

★   ★   ★

PATRICK KILBRIDE had just made himself a pot of tea. He switched on the television set in the corner of the room, in time for the seven o' clock news on TV-am, walked into the little kitchen and picked up the teapot.

He now lived in a rented room in Oldham, six miles from the Ashton council house where he and Sheila had raised their seven children, five boys and two girls, on his wages as a flagger. He still saw his children fairly regularly, having a pint or two with his lads and when he had had one too many the subject of his conversation, sometimes with a sadly-shaking head, more often with an angrily-clenched fist, always returned to his first-born, John, whose life had been taken by Ian Brady so long ago, when Pat was still a young man and before his marriage broke up.

Mr Kilbride, though a strict father, was loved by his children, who knew of the torment he had suffered and that he had been unable to bear the lifetime's burden with the same quiet dignity of their mother Sheila, who had tried to hide her grief, suppress her anger, from others.

His anger had been publicly displayed six years earlier after Myra Hindley's sister Maureen had died. The man who said he would wait outside the jail and kill her if ever she was released believed that the murderess would be at Maureen's funeral at a Manchester crematorium. He and Ann West had been involved in violent struggles with the police after spotting a slim blonde woman among the mourners, who actually turned out to be a member of the family of Bill Scott, the older man Maureen had married after her divorce from David Smith.

Now all the hatred that had simmered was coming to the boil again with the recent publicity surrounding Myra who, in fact, in the eyes of the law, had *not* killed his son. She had been found not guilty at her trial of killing John, but guilty of harbouring Brady knowing he had killed the boy, a crime for which she was given a long-since completed seven year sentence.

His thick hair now grey, Pat Kilbride had spent the past 21 years, since Brady and Hindley were arrested, nursing a hatred that had never subsided. The words he heard next that December morning broke into his thoughts and sent the rage surging through him. The cup of tea, half way to his mouth, froze as the voice of the TV newscaster told him, and the rest of Britain: "*The Moors Murderess, Myra Hindley is this morning on her way back to Saddleworth Moor...*"

He cursed and swore aloud, incredulous at the news, and then stung into action. He'd kill her. He'd bloody well kill her. *Her, there,* where his son, whose warm, mischievous smile he still saw every day, had been so callously buried.

He went into the kitchen, opened the cutlery drawer and took out a knife, pointed with a sharp, five-inch blade that could rip open a throat. *He'd kill her.*

He buttoned his coat and slipped the weapon into the inside pocket. Then he poured half the contents of a bottle of whisky into a beer bottle, screwed on the top and pushed it into the outside pocket.

It was still dark outside as he stepped into the street and walked through the stinging sleet towards the town centre taxi ranks. Where to? asked the driver. Patrick Kilbride opened the door, sank into the seat.

"Saddleworth."

THE taxi slowed at the junction with the A669 from Oldham and the A635 and crawled past the Pressmen, stamping their feet to try to keep warm, some of them huddled in a bus shelter and around the side of the closed Clarence pub, trying to dodge the squally showers of sleet, hail and snow. Ahead of the car, as the road began to climb away from Greenfield to the Moor the A635 was coned off and guarded by policemen in dripping waterproofs, men who would take no nonsense. The driver turned to his passenger. That was as far as they could go. Four quid, please.

Pat Kilbride fumbled for his change, paid him and stepped out into the half light. There must be some way of getting round those coppers. He walked slowly up the road towards the checkpoint and then his pace quickened as, going off to the right, he saw a lane, a track going downhill and skirting the road block. He'd try that and if anybody stopped him he'd say he was a worker at the reservoir down the hillside.

He turned off just before the road block and went, unchallenged, down the lane, stopping to take a swig of the warming liquid from his bottle, wiping his lips with the back of his hand, his resolved to kill Myra Hindley growing with each gulp. He told me later that he had tried to borrow a rifle from a friend when the return of Myra had first been rumoured, but the friend had refused.

How he imagined he would get close enough to her to use the small knife he carried as an effective weapon defied logic, but the father's passion for revenge knew no practicalities. The icy wind tugged at his overcoat, the sleet stung his face, but still he pressed on, climbing back now to the main road twisting above him over the whitened Pennine hillsides.

He could not have known it, but there were now 300 police officers on Saddleworth Moor, every one with orders to protect Myra Hindley with his pension. And as Pat Kilbride panted up the steep, rough incline, back to the A635, two miles from where he had gone around the first road block, he was unaware that, just around the next bend in the road – and not far from where his son had lain in a shallow grave in the peat for almost two years – there was a strategic longstop, another checkpoint.

It was too late when he spotted the policemen, and they spotted him. He swore to himself, but drew his breath and decided to try to brazen it out, attempting to put a purposeful stride into his aching legs, like that of a man going to work. The policemen shortened the distance between them by walking towards him. Sorry sir. He couldn't go any further. No arguments. Worked at the reservoir, did he? Well, the reservoir was down *there*, not up *here*.

Gently, a policeman took his arm. And, sobbing with frustration, Patrick Kilbride was turned back towards Greenfield. Just as over Crowther's Farm, not far from where he had tried to get past the barricade, came a noise that made him turn his head sharply. A whirring, clattering sound growing louder from above the sheet of mist. Then taking form, growing much louder, larger, before lowering itself in a squatting position on the moorland road. *He knew, he bloody well knew*.

A white and red Metropolitan Police helicopter.

THE icy wind drove the hail and sleet like tiny, painful spears into her face as she stepped down from the still-droning machine, her eyes half-closed against the onslaught. Once more she was standing, this time shakily, in the place that had made her heart beat so rapidly so long ago. As it was beating now.

She wore all black. But it was not the leather jacket, the tight trousers and high leather boots that she had often worn in another time on that Moor. Now she was dressed in bulky, unflattering heavy-duty police weatherproofs and a Balaclava helmet which she tugged up to cover most of her pale face against the winter weather she had last felt lash her cheeks when she was young. Only the eyes were visible, taking in the outlines of the landscape around her, the tumbledown dry-stone walls, built by long-dead craftsmen; twisted, rusting barbed wire fencing, with tufts of dirty grey fleece torn from the backs of lost, stumbling sheep fluttering from its sharp spurs.

She drew a long, deep breath and looked up along the A635 where she had so often driven her Mini, at the hills, now thinly dusted on their clumps of grass with a layer of Christmas snow, then towards the rocks on the skyline. And she remembered another Christmas long ago when she and Ian Brady had killed and buried, near those rocks, a little girl. Lesley Ann Downey.

The weather then had been like today. Nothing had changed. It was as if the world, the calendar, had stood still, been suspended in a time warp for the two decades and more she had been away. She was middle-aged now. But the girl would, in the minds and hearts of those who loved her, always be ten. The boy, John Kilbride, whose grave had been a few hundred yards away, would always be 12.

The face of Saddleworth Moor was unchanged. And it still held terrible secrets that she and Ian Brady had left with it.

The world had altered so much since she had been denied access to it. She wouldn't recognise the centre of Manchester, now, they had told her when they visited her in prison. She had missed so very much. Changing fashions, rising and falling hemlines, the Permissive Society, Flower Power, holidays on foreign, sun-kissed beaches, perhaps with her kids. She'd have loved ki...

The sleet, icy, smarting, that came in angry, hissing squalls, broke her thoughts. She looked at the policemen standing beside her, their ranks growing as vehicles arrived on the scene to join her at the spot where the helicopter had landed. Four Range Rovers, two Transit vans, two dog vans and two Land Rovers, one of them with its windows blacked out. The police were thinking about kids, too, youngsters whose mothers had not seen them for 20-odd years.

Still looking about her, she followed the policemen to the waiting vehicles their engines idling, waiting to take her to the mobile search headquarters. "Right, get in this one, please." She was helped into the back of a white Range Rover, the fourth in the convoy, not, as she might have expected, into the Land Rover with blacked-out windows. That was a decoy, another part of the elaborate security plan, as was the code used by the officers to transmit messages to each other.

She glanced at her companions, the six police officers

who got in with her. It was virtually impossible to tell one from the other. They were all dressed exactly like her. Even to their bullet-proof vests.

The convoy moved off, windscreen wipers flicking away the blowing snow as it climbed the hillside. Past the rocks on the left where Lesley Ann had been buried, the place, down the hillside on the right that had hidden the body of John. She had known that road so well and remembered it so well. For it had returned to her mind every day since *they* had first travelled it with their secrets of death. Then round the black and white steel crash barriers that had been there when she had been behind the wheel.

The moan of the wind rose to a scream outside as the sheltering rocks fell behind them. Her mouth was dry, partly from the nervous, adrenalin-pumping sensation of the flight – something she had not felt since, as a girl, she rode on the 'Bobs' roller-coaster at Belle Vue amusement park in Gorton. But mainly because she had been so close to someone she had not seen – and nor had anyone else – for 23 years, five months and four days.

Pauline Reade.

SHE leaned back in her seat, twisting her head and rubbing the steamy window with the back of her woollen-gloved hand, staring until the place slipped from view. Now they were on the long, straight road of the high plateau, miles and miles of moorland on either side, stretching as far as the eye could see on a clear day, with no other part of the earth in view, like the edge of the world.

The convoy gathered speed then, approaching the lay-by where the Pressmen, locked inside the cordon, were waiting, watching, craning their necks as the vehicles approached. She crouched to the floor, out of camera lens view as they sped by, swishing through the slush. Then a left-hand turn, taking the road towards Meltham, and into the big quarry lay-by.

The young bobbies, many of whom had been in short trousers when Myra Hindley had last been on Saddleworth Moor, could not help but be curious as, with Detective Chief Superintendent Topping, Michael Fisher, a Home Office official and her two prison guards, she climbed the steps to the incident room, the operational control headquarters.

The face they saw, that not so long ago had belied its years, had been youthful, now looked so *old*. It seemed that the strain of the events leading up to her being there had aged her, etched the wrinkles into her features in a matter of months. So that was *her*. What the papers would give for *this* picture. But there were no cameras, except for the official ones. Every officer had been warned sternly about the consequences.

Why? wondered the junior coppers. Why, after more than 21 years of denials had this ageing woman returned and broken that long, long silence? Her motives probably mattered little to their seniors. They were looking for two graves.

Myra Hindley was also looking for two things, two priceless possession, she had lost on Saddleworth Moor.

Her freedom. And her soul.

Chapter Ten

PLEASE LET ME STAY...

THE vast, eerie landscape of Saddleworth Moor had for many, always been a place to fear, a no-man's land of fable. Up there, on that silent Pennine ridge, frightened hill farmers of a bygone century had carried lucky charms in their pockets to protect them from the vile spirits, the devil's disciples who, they believed, haunted the gaunt, barren wilderness.

Strange, unaccountable things are said to have happened to people in its awesome stillness. The Reverend Charles Zouche, who had been vicar of Saddleworth, blinded, with a white-hot stick, the landlady of the Cross Keys Inn at Uppermill, turning on her like a madman as she went to comfort him when he seemed in distress. No-one knew what motivated the normally mild-mannered clergyman. All that was known was that he had just returned, alone, from a walk on the Moor.

That was two centuries ago, but even in the twentieth century the grey, silent atmosphere of Saddleworth Moor still seems to affect those who go there. David Smith, who had been taken there two decades ago by the Moors Murderers, once told me: "That place gives me the creeps. Up there you have this funny feeling that there is no-one, nothing, but you, the earth and the sky. And then, in the wind, you can hear voices."

This place, then, that released men's fears and superstitions and, some believe, their evil, had been the playground of Myra Hindley, and today she had returned, like a wicked child, looking for its long-lost playthings. It seemed like a grotesque game of hide and seek in which she had now changed sides and joined the seekers.

The messages crackled over the airwaves between the control centre and the ring of marksmen, sheltering from the weather – now lessening to bad-tempered flurries, with the light improving – behind canvas windbreaks on the open moorland. *All clear*. Topping looked at the woman in her black, bulky clothing. *Ready*? It was no game to him. He could still see the faces of Joan Reade and Winnie Johnson.

Myra had said little since she had left her cell at Cookham Wood. The helicopter flight had been scary, the first time she had been in the air, like a bird, but not so free. And she had been glad of the brief respite when it had touched down at the private airfield of British Aerospace at Woodford, just outside Stockport, for refuelling, and a hot cup of coffee.

She had gazed through the window, when the journey had resumed down at Stockport's rooftops. Gorton would be over there, to the left. And what had once been Bannock Street. Then Hattersley, Wardle Brook Avenue, to the right. Wonder what it's like, now...?

Number 16 Wardle Brook Avenue, the address that she and Ian Brady had made one of the most infamous in Britain, was, in fact, unoccupied. The house where little Lesley Ann Downey had made her last, tape-recorded, pitiful pleas for mercy, for her life; the house whose walls had been splattered with the blood of Edward Evans, their final sacrifice to evil, had not had a tenant for more than a year. Nobody wanted to live there. A succession of departing, disturbed occupants had claimed it was haunted. Incurable dampness, like tears, streamed down its walls, screams had been heard in the night and the outline of a figure, swore the terrified families, had been seen lying on a bed. Even the intervention of an exorcist priest had failed to remove the curse.

Ian Brady and Myra Hindley had transferred, to an ordinary red-brick council house, the aura of fear and evil that enveloped Saddleworth Moor, the place that had loomed through the mist ten miles beyond Hattersley after the helicopter had left the city suburbs, the towns and the villages far behind. Number 7 Bannock Street had long ago been flattened by the bulldozers, Number 16 Wardle Brook Avenue was empty. Only Saddleworth Moor remained untouched by time. How well would she remember it? And the spots in particular in which the police were interested?

She had so far admitted nothing, no involvement with murders or even burials. She had just declared a willingness to co-operate, whatever the consequences. She had been careful to say that the places she had identified for Topping from the photographs and maps had been "of particular interest to *Ian Brady*, some of which I visited with him."

It had seemed a clever side-step, but it had not worked. For her public statement of remorse following the letter from Mrs Johnson and her "co-operation" with the police appeared to have failed to gain her a shred of sympathy in her quest for freedom. A cynical view would be that her motive now was to make people ask themselves: "Surely, if she had been involved she wouldn't take this risk of providing the evidence of *habeas corpus* against *herself*?" But one question would always be there. How, if her involvement had been as minimal as she seemed to suggest, did the bodies of the victims get to the Moor? Ian Brady didn't drive a car.

Up there, in that helicopter, heading north-east, then descending, towards Crowther's Farm, the features of Saddleworth Moor, flecked with white and looking, from the air, like a desert, almost lunar-like, touched by man only by the ribbon of the A635, had meant nothing to Myra.

It was reasonable to assume that when she and Brady had gone to the Moor for their more sinister purposes the visits would have been made in the cover of darkness or the frequently-descending mist. So how the hell after all those years, wondered some, was she going to pinpoint two tiny graves in this huge area that even in daylight presented her with what seemed a needle-in-a-haystack-situation?

Topping, however, remained unshaken in his conviction that she *could* help. What she had told him tallied with his suspicions of where the graves might be. He had tried, without her, to follow in the footsteps of that long-cold path of evil that she and Brady had taken together. Now he had her where he wanted her: by his side on Saddleworth Moor.

She shivered as they stepped outside into the raw wind, jerking the Balaclava up over her face. The white and red helicopter that had been her transport, was skimming the A635, its searchlight blazing through the haze, its pilot scanning the ground for any figure that should not be there. Not one chance was being taken. Nobody was going to spy on Myra, either through the lens of a camera or the sights of a gun.

They walked onto the Moor, the hard road surface beneath her feet being replaced by the spongy peat whose feel she could still remember from where *he* had been beside her. Now it was Peter Topping. She was seeking, with a new partner, what she had hidden with an old one. The poacher turned gamekeeper, the baddie turned – she hoped people would think – goodie.

It seemed unreal. She had spent almost half her life behind bars for what she and Ian Brady had done, for the cruel game they had started when they were young. Now, in her middle age, she was helping another man to finish it. She looked at her new partner.

"This way. *I think*."

BEYOND Hollin Brow Knoll where, 21 years earlier, they had found Lesley Ann, lay a vast sweep of landscape, Wessenden Head Moor, an area treated with great respect and caution by the most experienced of moorland walkers because of its treacherous conditions, even in summer.

Kenneth Oldham, MBE, a leading expert on the Pennine Way, recalling the original search of Saddleworth Moor, said in his book *The Pennine Way* that walkers "will not fail to be impressed by the ability of the police in finding anything at all from this overwhelming morass." And author Alan Binns who also knows the gruelling trek intimately, concurred in his book *Walking the Pennine*

Way: "One of the wonders of this case was that the bodies were ever discovered."

Binns, who took several parties of youngsters along the 250-mile footpath, recalled: "At *this* place I had the experience of almost losing one of my schoolboys who had a foolish theory that if you ran fast enough over the patches of bog you reached the other side before you sank in. This worked for a while until he ran into a bigger stretch and, far beyond reach of firm ground, sank to his waist. Only a frantic buckling together of belts and straps to form a rope prevented him from going under and it took a long time to cut enough sods of turf to make me a precarious series of stepping stones to reach him. Pulling him out almost dislocated his hips..."

This was the place where the squad, with its Guide, was now walking, a place of significance to the police investigators of the 1960s. For then, after the arrest of Ian Brady, they had found in his wallet, tucked under the dashboard of Myra's car, three sheets of white ruled paper containing, in code, what was later described as his 'Plan for Murder'. It was the meticulous Brady's method of covering their tracks after a killing, to ensure that no suspicions had been aroused. And that nothing had been disturbed in the spot where a victim had been buried.

In his notes, alongside an entry: *"Object: Reconnaissance; Detail: Check periodically to see if unmoved"* were the initials W/H. At first the detectives had thought that had been an abbreviation of Woodhead, another moorland spot five miles south down the Pennines that Brady and Hindley used to visit. But they later discovered it meant Wessenden Head, an area too immense to continue searching without further clues. But the bobbies of 1986 had Myra Hindley with them...

Wessenden Head was a place whose rocks had been blackened with soot carried by rain from the chain of mill towns, in the days when they had prospered in the valley below, a place where the red grouse had called to Myra Hindley when she was young, with an unmistakable cry, she wished she had heeded: *"Go back, go back."*

The party – two of its members carrying a stretcher, for it was possible that their Guide's physical condition might not stand up to the rigors – plodded on across the open, unsheltered moorland, where the moan of the wind that tore at their clothing had reached a high-pitched scream and the mist was at its densest. Topping brought out his map and, alongside his loyal lieutenant, newly-promoted Chief Inspector Geoff Knupfer, ran his finger over the wildly-flapping page. Myra had stopped, a mile from the road, reckoned the policemen. That was a long, long way to carry a body. *Unless...* They let the thought go for the moment.

She seemed bewildered, apparently annoyed with herself and now, with *them*, the media. For encircling the area, in that leaden sky over the moors, were four other helicopters, chartered by the Press and TV, edging closer in the forlorn hope of getting a glimpse of the woman, the murderess. For the next few minutes the airwaves were peppered with colourful language and air traffic control chipped in to warn the pilots they were breaking low-flying rules. Topping, as always, outwardly unruffled, shrugged and looked at Myra. She gestured hopelessly. She wasn't sure. It was all so long ago. But she *could* help, given time. She thought they'd come the wrong way. She'd try again.

There were two other men besides the policemen and prison officers in the party of black-clad figures – her solicitor, Michael Fisher and the man from the Home Office, sent there by Douglas Hurd to keep an official eye on his charge. The murderess called to her solicitor and whispered to him. Bring over the Home Office man, she wanted to talk to him. She wanted to *tell* him. She knew what people were thinking.

The official trudged through the peat and looked quizically at Myra. The eyes through the slit in the Balaclava stared at him intently. Listen, she said, there was one thing she wanted to make clear. It was something she had been thinking about for some time, months. Topping was looking at his watch. Above them the media helicopters, now joined in the sky by the Met chopper trying to keep them at bay, were still circling. *The media.* They'd make something of this. She looked down at her gum-booted feet, sinking in the black, snow-peppered earth, and told him, hoarsely that she knew the question of her parole would next be reviewed in 1990. And that she didn't want to be considered.

Forget it.

MYRA looked up again at the official. She needed more time here. It had been half her lifetime ago. Let her stay on longer than a day. One day wasn't enough. *Please.* He shook his head firmly. No. She must be back at Cookham Wood tonight. Her agitation was clearly growing. She had said she didn't want considering for parole. Nobody could say she was after doing a deal. *Why?* NO. Topping knew that time was of the utmost importance. They had little enough of it and it would be going dark in another three hours. His men would go on looking, dig, here. Let's press on.

The convoy was waiting at the roadside to take them back to the control centre for lunch, a hurried affair, Topping's eyes constantly straying to his relentlessly-ticking watch, Myra nibbling moodily, like a spoilt child, at the sandwiches that had been packed by the canteen ladies at Greater Manchester Police headquarters.

Topping's men, meanwhile, had been dealing swiftly, efficiently and, perhaps for those who fell foul of them, a little frighteningly with any attempts to break through their cordon. The intrepid Paul Callan and his colleague Stephen White of the *Daily Mirror* had slogged five miles to try to spot Myra before being surrounded by police and commanded, at gunpoint, to lie face down in the cold, sticky peat. They were searched from head to toe, handcuffed and ordered into a police van, to be taken back to Greenfield in as many minutes as they had taken hours to get to the Moor.

And on the Pennine Way, two puzzled young hikers, a boy and a girl, had their journey interrupted by the armed officers. Sorry, they couldn't go any further. Would they get in the van, please...? It was Myra's Moor for the day.

So elaborate had been the security operation that the Press in the valley, waiting at the lay-by, those in the helicopters, had not accurately tracked the movements of Myra Hindley. A number of decoy parties, none of them including her, had been sent out on the Moor. The photographers in the air were certain they had pinpointed the killer, distinguished by her red mittens. And *Today* newspaper triumphantly carried a huge front-page picture next day, in colour, the scarlet gloves standing out vividly. They were, however, on the hands of a young policewoman in one of the sham patrols.

The real search party had less than half an hour for lunch before setting out again, this time from a different direction, across Wessenden Head Moor, towards a place called Shiny Brook, a place where, at night, the water of the nearby reservoirs had glistened with the reflection of the moon. A place, it now seemed, where evil had been performed.

Her legs ached, but she walked on, stumbling occasionally in her clumsy boots on the rough ground, until they reached a gully. *Here.* There was a wide sweep, a very wide sweep of the arm. Was she sure? One gully looked pretty much the same as another. She had taken them the wrong way once, admitted she was lost. Was she really sure?

She looked back, the way they had come, remembering a walk of, perhaps, 22 years ago and possibly other walks (..."*check periodically to see if unmoved...*") along the same route. At last, for the first time since 1965, the police had narrowed down an area of Wessenden Head Moor. The official police photographer's camera would click there many times. Topping would want to compare pictures of the gully with those from the tartan-backed album that had yielded the vital clues to the detectives of a generation ago.

In the valley, at the roadblock, shivering with cold, but determined to be as close as possible to the incredible activity high above them, two mothers had stood, Ann West and Winnie Johnson, and had pleaded with the police officers to be allowed to go on the Moor. It was, of course, totally out of the question and they knew it. There was, as always, the hate, the bitter suspicion in Mrs West's heart. "*She's* on a day out," she said. "Does she think she's going to get parole? She won't while I'm alive."

Mrs Johnson, though, had been praying that the woman who said she had been touched by her heart-rending plea for help would be able to lead them to her son. Her desire to have him laid in a final resting place, to know just where he was, outweighed any scorn or anger she might have felt. Paul Reade, who had searched so frantically for his sister through those Manchester backstreets more than 23 years ago, was there too, sharing the feelings and hopes of Mrs Johnson. For he knew that only Myra Hindley and Ian Brady could ease the suffering of his family, particularly that of his mother, now an extremely sick woman.

Joan Reade sat in her council house living room in Openshaw, two miles from her former home where she had last seen Pauline alive. She was pale and drawn, not fully recovered from a severe attack of shingles. "I have a feeling, a mother's feeling, that my daughter is up on those moors," she said quietly. "All I want is to get her away from there, so she can have a decent burial."

Meanwhile, Patrick Kilbride had had a stern warning from the police. He had tried yet again to break through the police barricade by climbing over a church wall in the village and had been stopped as he tried to slip around the roadblock. The police, sympathetic, yet firm, cautioned him. By this time two of his sons, Danny, now 34 and Terry, 31, had joined him, suspecting that he would have been unable to stay away from the place where his son, their brother, had been buried.

They found him still distraught, a little the worse for drink, sitting in the Clarence pub, his eyes moist from the tears of frustration. "I just shook when I heard on TV that

that woman was going up there," he said. "I still don't know how my son died and that is eating the heart out of me."

I had been one of the journalists at the roadblock and had seen Mr Kilbride go into the Clarence. I knew the family well and had first met the tortured father on that November day in 1963 when the police were looking for his eldest son, never imagining that he had been caught up in the unbelievable web of evil spun by Brady and Hindley.

I followed them into the pub and sat on the chair opposite Mr Kilbride. He put down his glass heavily and looked at me, his eyes red-rimmed. "All this is eating the heart out of me," he repeated. "It broke up my marriage, ruined my life. Because of this lot, *her* and *him*, I just went haywire. I became an alcoholic." He shook his head and pushed his hand into his inside pocket, pulling out the knife with which he had armed himself that morning. "This is what I came to do." His hand shook as he raised the weapon, small, but lethal. "I'd like to cut *her* to ribbons." He sobbed. "I just want her dead."

Danny, whose mother had begged him to stay away, broke in. "No, dad. She's got a job to do up there. She..." The increased volume of the TV in the corner of the lounge bar drowned his words. The one o'clock news was starting and on the screen were pictures of the Moor above us. Aerial views of the cold winter-coated hillsides were now going into living rooms all over Britain. And into a room at Park Lane Hospital, Liverpool, whose occupant, his lips a tight line, his eyes cold, hard, had every bit as much interest as Patrick Kilbride in the activities of Myra Hindley.

Ian Brady.

SHE took the policeman's outstretched hand and stepped gingerly, now with the caution of a middle-aged woman, across the rotten wooden plank that formed a makeshift bridge over the sludge-filled ditch. Myra had been only 23 when she last crossed that roadside obstacle, then with the confidence of youth. Now she was older than most of the policemen, around two dozen of them, some with rifles slung over their shoulders, who surrounded her.

OK? asked Topping, by her side. She nodded and the group pressed on, up the hillside, trying to keep to the tufts of pale grass that provided stepping stones through the peat. She looked up at the stark winter skyline and stopped, pausing for breath, turning her head to prevent the icy wind snatching her words before they could reach the ears of the CID chief. "A bit further on."

They were now at Hollin Brow Knoll. They had spent most of the day at Shiny Brook, a long trek that had left her exhausted, her legs like lead. But she had not needed that stretcher. It had served instead as a conveyance for one of the women prison officers who had accompanied her and had slipped and twisted her ankle – an incident, it was said later, that provided Myra Hindley with the only light relief of the day.

Shiny Brook had been so vast. If only she could remember properly. If only she could have longer... But, with the light fading Topping had asked her to take them to the other place she had mentioned, Hollin Brow Knoll.

The convoy had roared over the Moor to that partly submerged plank across the ditch. They had climbed up the hillside, their figures dimly silhouetted against the darkening skyline, the Press and TV helicopters, now restricted to a higher altitude because of stern warnings from Air Traffic Control, still clattering overhead.

The road was behind them, the rocks of Hollin Brow Knoll to their left. *Further on*. They reached the top of the ridge, some 100, perhaps 150 yards from the A635. *A bit further*. She glanced over her shoulder, the road was just out of sight. She walked on a few yards and stopped. *Around here. It was in this area*. She pointed vaguely, her arm again moving in a wide arc, backwards and forwards. She nodded emphatically. She was *sure* it was *around here*...one of the places that had been *"of particular interest to Ian Brady,"* that is... She looked around her again, measuring with her eye, her mind, the distance from the hilltop, from the rocks.

Again the memory of a long-ago summer night, eleven days before her twenty-first birthday, returned. She pointed, this time with more certainty, with more agitation, towards the ground. Just give her a bit more time. She *could* do it, she *could* help them. *Another day...please.*

The CID chief would have liked her to have been given another day, too. But he knew the rules. He was a servant to them, bound by them. If Douglas Hurd had said one day he meant just that and not a minute more. But Myra again turned on the man from the Home Office. She tore down the Balaclava covering her mouth. "Let me come back tomorrow. Keep me in a police station overnight, or at Styal Prison," she pleaded, referring to the women's jail in Cheshire. Again the official was emphatic. No way.

Her shoulders slumped, then shook. Tears began to trickle down her face. She started to sob. Then, in the shadow of Hollin Brow Knoll, where a little girl who had begged *her..."please, mummy"...*had been buried, so close to the place of another dreadful secret of death, she broke down and cried.

Half an hour later, with the sky over Saddleworth Moor now black with night, the snow still mantling its gaunt hillsides, she was on her way back to jail, to continue her briefly interrupted life sentence. And leaving behind her an intriguing question: Why had she wanted to remain there? Was she really so anxious to help the police she had scorned for 21 years and the families of two missing children? The policemen who had been with her believed she was. But she had also tasted the honey of her lost youth that day.

The roadblocks had been lifted and Topping was telling reporters that he and Myra had done their best in the time available. He was surprised that she had been able to recall so much and she had given him and his men two new areas to look at. He was not unhappy. And, no, he didn't think she'd be going back to the moors.

Down in the valley the children had arrived safely home from school. A day nearer Christmas, Santa Claus, turkey, mince pies, holly, mistletoe, toys, the pantomime to look forward to at Tameside Theatre or Oldham Coliseum.

High above them, a helicopter was veering south with a tearful woman in one of its passenger seats, knowing the cynics would be asking if *this* had all been a charade, a pantomime. Whatever her reasons for wanting to stay longer than the seven and a half hours she had spent on the Moor she would be back in her lonely cell tonight. For her, like Cinderella, the ball was over.

And she was still the Wicked Fairy.

THROUGHOUT that day Ian Brady had watched the news bulletins on his television screen, looking intently for a glimpse of the woman who had been by his side there, and had stood beside him for the last time on Friday, 6 May 1966 in the dock on the final day of their trial. She could have been any one of the vague, shadowy figures walking in the mist. He gazed at the moors, looking for familiar outlines. Where had she taken them? Were they any closer to *the secrets?*

He had switched on his radio every hour, too, to listen for developments and that night had talked to his lawyer, Benedict Birnberg, on the 'phone. He had, said Mr Birnberg, been "non-committal" about the day's events. The man who knew so much, the murderer, was keeping his secrets to himself. It was obvious that, with the worsening winter weather, there was little chance of any discovery by the police until the spring. There was time to plan his strategy, his next move in the game with Myra Hindley. He would wait. Don't get mad. *Get even.*

The next day the papers were full of it and, inevitably, there were the barbs from members of parliament, one of whom called it an expensive publicity stunt. And Geoffrey Dickens declared: "Myra Hindley's murders were the most heinous of the century. I hope that this and future home secretaries will not be hoodwinked by any cooperation from her." His Conservative colleague Peter Bruinvels was even more caustic: "I think they are barmy to let her out at all. Once she has tasted freedom she will reckon she is in line for parole." The Home Secretary, however, promised there would be no deals.

Topping wished the critics would get off his back. He returned to the Moor to investigate the spots pointed out by Myra. *Nothing.* He had David Smith brought from his new, secret address in the Midlands, to see if a tour of the area would jog his memory. *Nothing.*

The snowfalls were getting worse. By now drifts three feet deep were clogging the gullies. Reluctantly Topping had to say it. OK, let's call it a day.

He reported to the waiting Pressmen: "The digging has stopped and will not be restarted until the spring when it gets warmer. Temperature is vital for us to be able to use the search dogs. Meantime we will be evaluating information we have gathered so that we will be able to pinpoint specific areas to search when we return. Myra Hindley's visit was very useful and I am hoping to see Ian Brady again." He allowed himself, uncharacteristically, a slight pat on the back. "We are temporarily leaving the operation with our tails high and in a more optimistic frame of mind than before." Then he left Saddleworth Moor with his men. Thanks lads. Oh, and Merry Christmas.

Next morning Ian Brady put down the newspapers and nodded to himself. Winter had beaten them. And Myra.

There had been an item in the newspapers that he may have missed for, amid the drama of 'The Return' it had not been given great prominence, but it was an indication of the great evil, the terror that still surrounded him and Myra Hindley. On the very day she went back to Saddleworth Moor a decision was taken by the housing committee in Manchester, to demolish one of its properties, a house, the end of a row, for which they could not get a tenant.

Number 16 Wardle Brook Avenue, Hattersley.

Chapter Eleven

THE CONFESSION

THE criticism against the police operation was mounting. Saddleworth Moor was now sealed off by the snow of winter and Topping was helpless to take the practical action that might result in silencing his critics, one of whom described the inquiry as a gruesome charade...ghoulish, over-dramatised and almost indecent.

There was even a demand that a senior police officer from another force should be called in to examine the situation and decide, with the Home Secretary, whether there were sufficient new facts to justify the investigation going on. Otherwise, the whole thing should be called off, and the files closed, once and for all.

The return had cost £12,000 said the Home Office – a figure that was challenged by Labour MP Mr Doug Hoyle. "This figure cannot be right because, for a start, we have already been told by the Home Office that 1,590 hours of police overtime were worked on this ludicruous venture," he fumed. "I want precise details of every item of the cost of this botched and inefficient operation conducted at the wrong time of the year and which, among other things, was a factor in the departure of Mr John Stalker, the Deputy Chief Constable of Greater Manchester."

At that time, Greater Manchester police had been under the spotlight because of the publicity surrounding Mr Stalker who, in fact, had been involved, as a young officer, with the original Moors Murders case. He had been taken off an inquiry he was conducting over 'shoot to kill' allegations against the Royal Ulster Constabulary following allegations against him that he had associated with Manchester criminals. He cleared himself completely of the smears, but decided to retire eight years early. Now it was being suggested that the great 'pantomime' on the moors had been staged to divert public attention away from the Stalker affair – a charge strongly denied by Topping.

It was also being claimed that one of the factors that led to the Deputy Chief Constable's decision to leave his post was that, despite his high rank, he had not been told about Myra's return to the Moor. The first he had known of it was when he heard the news on his radio that morning. There is little doubt that Stalker, a dedicated policeman, had been hurt by this, just as Topping, equally dedicated, was hurt by the jibes.

It was painfully frustrating for the detective, who felt he was so close to a breakthrough. He had two places now lined up in his sights – the area near Hollin Brow Knoll and, two miles away, Shiny Brook. But he knew it might be months before he could return to the Pennines to put the worth of Myra Hindley's visit to the test.

He had no choice but to wait. It was a long, long winter, in which there were record-breaking low temperatures. During the cold months a date passed which broke one mother's heart and was a jolting reminder of just how long it had been.

February 18, 1987. Pauline Reade would have been forty.

AT last it was spring. The snow on Saddleworth Moor had melted, with water running in streams down its hillsides, rivulets trickling down the inclines of the A635. And Peter Topping and his men were back there. The Press returned. Snoopy's caravan cafe was back in full business on the big lay-by close to the Greater Manchester–West Yorkshire boundary, serving mugs of tea and bacon sandwiches to the media men, hungry, too, for a new story.

But Topping was to catch every one of them – plus those who had kept a vigil at Cookham Wood – and all their news editors, napping. For, on Tuesday, 24 March 1987, without a soul outside the police force and the Home

Office knowing about it, he had taken Myra Hindley back to the Moor.

It was two days after she was safely back in her cell that the journalists found out about the new visit. The CID chief confirmed it, but he would say nothing further. Both he and Douglas Hurd had been determined that her return should this time be in the strictest secrecy. Not even Myra's solicitor had known.

The police had first gone back to the Moor at the beginning of the month. It was a low-key operation, with a handful of officers digging and probing the now-softened peat in the Shiny Brook area, and Topping saying: "I am confident that we will be successful at the end of the day."

The news editors yawned. Oh yeah? Then suddenly, on the night of Friday, 6 March, the apparently futile efforts of a seemingly obsessed policeman paled into insignificance against a news story that rocked the world. A ferry, the Herald of Free Enterprise, just setting out from Zeebrugge for Britain, capsized. More than 180 people were dead or missing. Forget Peter Topping, forget Saddleworth Moor. The news desks were getting sceptical, anyway. The story was all but dead.

There were plenty of other events to fill the newspapers and take up air time on TV and radio: a Budget that had left cigarettes, drink and petrol prices unchanged, Irangate, the jailing of the killers of PC Trevor Blakelock, a General Election in the offing. And, with the total rising by seven per cent, a record year for crime – a fact that could not fail to attract the attention and possible criticism of those who felt that the Detective Chief Superintendent was wasting his time.

Topping had chosen a good time to take the murderess back to the moors, just when Press interest was flagging and when news editors had decided they could no longer afford the luxury of having men staked out in the Pennines on the off chance of a new development in the story.

On the night of Monday, 23 March, under a prison release order bearing the signature of the Home Secretary,

Myra Hindley was driven from Cookham Wood to Manchester. This time, said Mr Hurd, there was to be no media circus.

She was taken in the unmarked car to spend two nights – her first outside prison since her arrest in 1965 – at the Greater Manchester police training school in the Prestwich area. It was the first time she had lain down her head in her native city since she was 23. Her sleeping accommodation was the cheerfully decorated flat normally used by the officer in charge of the establishment. Every door, every window, every corridor was bolted, sealed and guarded.

Topping and a handful of his men took her back to the two key locations she had pointed out in December, spending most of their time at Shiny Brook. This time the roads were not closed, there was no ring of armed men. And no Pressmen. But even had there been reporters and photographers keeping an eye on the situation as they had for weeks, they would have been none the wiser. For with Myra dressed in the same casual attire as the police officers, the scene of activity appeared to be exactly the same as it had since the beginning of the month: just a few bobbies walking around and prodding in the peat. There was no fuss, no drama, with Topping at her side, looking, listening. Taking her back had been of vital importance to the detective and he had convinced the Home Secretary that Myra, who three months earlier had pleaded to stay on, could make a valuable contribution to his investigation.

By the time the news leaked out it was too late. She was back inside Cookham Wood, "exhausted," said her solicitor, "but glad she could continue to be of help." Mr Geoffrey Dickens commented: "I hope Mr Topping is not being hoodwinked by this evil bitch who likes a taste of freedom, even just for a few hours."

But Topping stuck to his guns. "There *are* bodies on the Moor. There is no doubt about that," he said. "I remain convinced I will find them." There was no doubt that he had learned much, much more from Myra Hindley than he was prepared to say.

For now, he and his small squad of men were searching the Moor for one of the murderers' secrets with metal detectors.

What *were* they looking for? Topping refused to say beyond: "We are searching for something which would be a great help to the inquiry, but it is not a body." There was speculation that they were seeking a metal box containing perhaps more tell-tale photographs that had been hidden by Brady. And, said the detective, finding the clue "would be an important part of the jigsaw and has come as a result of my many interviews with Myra Hindley."

Something else had come as a result of his many interviews with her during that seemingly unproductive winter, something detectives of 21 years ago would never have believed would happen, something that would have the bored editors re-scheming the front pages of their newspapers.

A confession of murder from Myra Hindley.

IT was the eve of the Grand National and I was at the Aintree racecourse at Liverpool to write a piece for my paper, *The Star*, on the last-minute preparations, scenes of excitement, as the stage was set for the world's greatest steeplechase. It was a bitterly cold day, the wind sweeping across the famous turf and moaning as it sought an escape in the empty grandstands.

The weather would have been twice as bad on Saddleworth Moor, but Peter Topping and his tiny army would be there, he on his hands and knees in the squelching peat, his waterproofs spattered with mud, searching, it seemed, every grain of the black soil. A senior colleague had been quoted as saying: "His whole life now seems to revolve around solving this case. He is certain he will find remains on that Moor." But scepticism about the operation was still growing, and there were other stories for newspapermen to think about. Like the Grand National.

I had filed my story from Aintree and asked the copytaker to transfer my call to Jeff McGowan, my news editor. "I've just put over my copy," I began. "I'll..." McGowan who, as a young reporter for the *Daily Express* had covered the original, horrendous story of the moors, interrupted. "Never mind about that. What about *this*?" He had, in front of him on his desk, an agency story. *Myra Hindley had said she could no longer live a lie. She was as guilty as Ian Brady.*

The words of her confession, penned in the loneliness of her cell, had been read out by Michael Fisher to the world. They were chilling. And damning.

"When I was arrested, tried and convicted I was still obsessed and infatuated with Ian Brady. I could not bring myself to admit the truth about our crimes. Between 1966 and 1977 I served my sentence at Holloway Prison. There I did what I could to hide the truth from myself and from others, believing this was the only way I could survive the ordeal of a very long prison sentence. From 1977 to 1983 I served my sentence in Durham where I became completely ostracised from the outside world, living a totally unreal life with 30 or so life and long-term women prisoners. I was aware that public hostility towards me was, if anything, increasing and I reacted by withdrawing more and more into myself.

"In 1983 I was transferred to Cookham Wood prison. This move was interpreted by some as a first step towards my eventual release, but I knew this was simply an alternative prison for me. Since I have been here, I have received considerable help and encouragement which has strengthened my resolve and I began to become more confident that I could be open and frank about my case. Throughout my sentence I have been haunted by the continued suffering of the relatives of the two children who were missing at the time of my arrest and until recently I have been utterly overwhelmed by the numerous difficulties of revealing the truth.

"I have had to consider the consequences for my family who have suffered far more than I have and I have been fearful of the effect that facing up to the truth would have on me and my existence in prison, which has always been a tremendous ordeal. In 1985, under the personal direction of a Jesuit from Farm Street, I continued the Ignatian Spiritual exercises which I began in Durham Prison with the Jesuit chaplain. These spiritual exercises lasted over a year and gave me great strength and brought me closer to God than I have ever been before. It was then that I realised I could no longer live a lie. The former prison governor, Peter Timms, now a Methodist minister, agreed to help with the task ahead. His experience of dealing with life sentence prisoners and their cases has been invaluable.

"On the 31st October, 1986, I received a letter from Mrs Johnson, begging for help. This was the first such letter I had ever received and on the 18th November, I resolved to assist the Greater Manchester Police, who had reopened the case of the two missing children. I felt able to cooperate with the officer leading that inquiry, Detective Chief Superintendent Topping, whose approach to me was professional, but kind and sympathetic.

"I was taken to the moors a few weeks later and did what I could to identify the places where I believed the two children were buried. However, this visit was frustrated by the enormous Press interest and by the weather.

"It was to Peter Timms that I first was able to make a full admission of guilt and immediately afterwards, I instructed my solicitor to contact Chief Superintendent Topping who attended at the prison with his assistant, Detective Inspector Knupfer, to hear my voluntary statement on the 19th, 20th, 23rd and 24th February. In this statement, I admitted my role in these awful events and said that I considered myself to be as guilty as my former lover, Ian Brady, although our roles were different.

"Later, I was taken to the moors secretly and out of the glare of publicity I was able to be far more specific about the location of graves and I now believe that I have done all that I can in helping the police in this respect. I know that the parents of the missing children may never be able to forgive me, and that words of mine can NEVER express the remorse I now feel for what I did and my refusal for so long to admit to the crimes. I hope that my actions now that I am making my confession to the police will speak louder than any words. I want nothing more than to help the police find the bodies so that their poor relatives can at last have the comfort of giving them a Christian burial.

"To those who believe that I am seeking some narrow advantage I would stress that I am in my 24th year of imprisonment, that my next parole review is not due until 1990, by which time I shall have served 26 years. I have informed the Home Office that I do not wish to be considered for release on parole in 1990, and for as far ahead as I can see I know I will be kept in prison."

Myra Hindley.

Not far from Aintree, in another part of Liverpool, Ian Brady, whose mental condition was said to be deteriorating, had also heard the news on the TV in his hospital room.

Now, I wondered, what would *his* next move be?

INEVITABLY, the question now being asked was: Will Myra Hindley – and Ian Brady – be brought to trial *again*? Would they, once more, in a bizarre repeat of history, stand together in the dock, now as a middle-aged couple, to answer further crimes of their youth?

Michael Fisher had warned Myra of the possible consequences, but he said she had been adamant to tell the world the secret with which she had said she had lived so long. "After sitting in on all of the prison interviews conducted by Mr Topping I have not the slightest doubt that the bodies of Keith Bennett and Pauline Reade will be found very quickly. I warned her she could be walking into a murder charge. She accepted the risk. Her message is that she wants to put an end to the case and at the same time do her public duty."

Her champion Lord Longford described the confession as "a very brave and fine statement that I would expect from Myra." But the families of her victims and members of parliament were demanding that she was returned to the dock, even though it seemed that this time it might be alone. For there were great doubts that Ian Brady would be considered mentally fit to plead.

There was now concern about his condition. He was said to be in a state of deep depression, confining himself to his room and he did not want to see visitors. Topping had said he was available to see him any time he liked and even the tormented Margaret Brady had urged her son to end the speculation. Even to stand trial if he had to.

But Ian Brady was keeping quiet. As silent as the graves on Saddleworth Moor that Peter Topping was determined to find.

The policeman was now on the Moor every day. Every morning he and his team of eight men arrived in a white van. They carried spades, trowels and metal detectors and trudged from the road to Shiny Brook where they set to work in a quiet, systematic pattern. The handful of Pressmen who remained on the Moor had by that time deduced that the metal detectors were being used to find the spade with which Ian Brady had dug the graves and that Topping knew that if he found that spade it would be very close to at least one of the burial places.

Their search method was to remove the top layer of peat that would have covered the ground over the past 20-odd years to see if there had been any disturbance in the ground beneath it. Every trowelful was replaced precisely at the request of the Peak District National park, anxious that the landscape should be conserved. Every day Topping went back, got on his hands and knees and spent hour after patient hour. Every night he was the last man to walk off the Moor, politely telling the reporters: "I am still confident" or "I am still hopeful."

And of his critics he would say: "They don't know what I know. God help us when we come to the day in this country when we don't investigate murder. I am still hopeful of a successful conclusion. I owe it to the public, the families, my profession and myself to do all I can.''

But he was having to admit that he could not go on indefinitely and that the resources and manpower he was using could not be sustained without results.

At the same time, pressure was mounting to put the now self-confessed murderess on trial. And if the law wouldn't do it a private prosecution could be taken out, said Tory MP Peter Bruinvels. Ann West told me at the time: ''If Hindley is not charged with murder I won't let it rest there. I will beg, if necessary, to get the money together to brief a barrister. It's all right to say that after her confession she will spend the rest of her life in jail anyway, but there is always the chance that she will be let out. I want to make sure that she stays where she is. I *still* believe there's method behind this apparent madness.''

There was another statement from Myra Hindley: ''I am prepared to stand trial, though what good reason it would serve – apart from satisfying the very understandable wishes of the relatives of the missing children – I cannot imagine. A trial would be another tremendous ordeal for my mother, who is also an innocent victim in all this, and for me. I feel as if I have been on trial for 22 years and whatever sentence a court may pass it will not exceed my expectation of life imprisonment.''

Meanwhile 250 miles away Peter Topping was still looking.

★   ★   ★

IT was just before Easter that I met Detective Chief Superintendent Peter Topping by the roadside near Shiny Brook. He had just spent another day on the Moor and he and his men were returning to their vehicle. I had gone up there out of curiosity. What was driving him, one of Britain's most senior detectives, to keep coming back here, every day, on what people were saying was a hopeless mission?

The wind was icy, pulling at his waterproof leggings and tweed trilby hat as we faced each other on the Moor. His greeting was polite and friendly, though I thought he looked a little tired. How was the investigation going? I asked. He was still hopeful of that successful conclusion. Was the strain of the sheer graft of it all beginning to tell on him? I wondered. He shrugged, smiled briefly. "It's keeping me fit."

I knew, though, that concentration on the same subject, particularly one such as this, was extremely wearing. While working on my book on the Moors Murders I had found it almost impossible to shut the topic from my mind. Saddleworth Moor had been the last place in my thoughts before I went to sleep and the first when I woke up. It had haunted me and I wondered if it was having the same effect on Peter Topping, posing the question in the story for *The Star* which I wrote after our meeting.

He 'phoned me a few days later, not angry, for that was not his nature. Just disappointed, he said, by my suggestion that he was caught up in the spell of the Moor. He felt it was a slur in his professionalism. That was the very last impression I had wanted to create, for Peter Topping was the complete professional who had achieved so much where others had failed.

He later told the Press Association: "No matter what people say, we aren't caught up in the spell of the moors and we have not got moors fever. I am a policeman in charge of a double murder inquiry after all is said and done. We are well into the programme that we planned at the beginning. The inquiry has gone a long way and we are still hopeful of finding the bodies. There are still one or two areas we want to have a look at and there is also another site which we will be looking at a mile or so away."

On Friday, 1 May 1987, for the first weekday for more than five weeks, the familiar nine-man chain gang failed to turn up on Saddleworth Moor. Puzzled journalists who contacted Greater Manchester Police headquarters were told that Mr Topping was "in conference" there.

The fact was that he was 40 miles from his office in Liverpool. He spent five hours talking to Ian Brady.

Chapter Twelve

THE FINDING OF PAULINE READE

THE sooty terraces, the cobbled streets of that corner of Manchester that had known such mystery and grief had long gone. There were no longer noisy children playing hide and seek in its warren of back streets, alleys and ginnals, or hopscotch on cracked pavement flags near the donkey-stoned doorsteps.

The exodus of Gorton of two decades ago of families and industries that provided their living, like its foundry and railway carriage works, had stripped it bare, leaving a heartless husk. There was no Wiles Street, no Bannock Street, just grassed, open ground flanked by council houses and planted here and there with saplings that would not have lasted five minutes with the boisterous young inhabitants of the 1960s.

The Steel Works Tavern was still there, standing alone in Gorton Lane, surviving the foundry with which its name was associated, one of the last reminders of a summer night in 1963, the last time anyone saw one of its young inhabitants, a teenage girl in a pretty pink dress. Pauline Reade.

Myra Hindley would not have recognised the place where she grew up, the place that, on 23 July 1942, spawned a monster.

Manchester, like most cities, had changed vastly. Many of its lofty Victorian buildings had now gone, to the dismay of a good many of its citizens, to be replaced by even loftier glass and concrete structures. The huge Arndale Centre now straddled Market Street where she and Ian Brady had window-shopped on Saturday afternoons when she had gazed at engagement rings in the jewellers' windows. C and A had moved into the Arndale Centre from Oldham Street, they no longer had waitress service in the restaurant at Lewis's store, the buses that used to be red were now orange and white and most of the night clubs that had earned Manchester a swinging city reputation had gone.

But one aspect of Manchester life to which its natives had clung was its traditional Whit Walks in May. Thousands of children, generation after generation, the girls in their new frocks, the boys in their new suits, with new pennies in the pockets for luck, have taken part in the religious festival, processions led by church elders as a demonstration of their faith, for longer than anyone can remember.

The tradition spreads well beyond Manchester and its suburbs, to the old mill towns that surround it like a necklace and to the villages on the roads climbing away, east, to the Pennines. The colourful processions, with banners bearing the names of the churches, are led by brass bands, often each church with a band of its own, engaged specially for the day. And each playing a different rousing march as they pass the thousands lining the pavements.

Many of the Whit Walks had taken place on Whit Friday, now no longer recognised as a public holiday in the Greater Manchester area and nowadays the processions are staggered on dates around mid-May. Whit Friday, however, is still the Big Day for the 10,000 inhabitants of the villages of Saddleworth, famed for their brass band contests, a day when the narrow streets become choked with people and traffic and the pubs are packed almost to suffocation.

Dozens of the same brass bandsmen who march ahead of the Walks also play in Uppermill and Dobcross, coachloads of them coming from the other side of the Pennines, from Black Dyke Mills, from Brighouse and Rastrick, from Hammond's Sauce Works, Yorkshiremen, cornetists, trombonists, euphoniumists, slaking their thirst with Lancashire ale and playing their hearts out for the judges.

In May 1987 the villages below Saddleworth Moor were preparing for the contests, their Whit Walks and, this year, for a coinciding event, the Saddleworth Festival, a pageant of music and folklore which would bring in visitors from all over Britain and beyond. But the people knew that Saddleworth was etched on the map of the world not for its music or the history of its villages, but for the twentieth century activities, high above them, of a woman from the city who had once demonstrated her Faith by marching behind the brass bands.

And their Member of Parliament was saying that the current activities of Peter Topping and his men were casting a dark, gloomy shadow over their lives. "The only reason the people of Saddleworth have been kind to Mr Topping is in respect for the feelings of the parents of the missing children. That's why we have held our tongues," said Mr Geoffrey Dickens. "Underneath we have had enough. If he really has got some concrete evidence then by all means carry on. But if he relies on Hindley I'm afraid he has been hoodwinked and bitten the bait.

"On the day he left the moors last week for the first time on a normal working day he went to see Brady for further questioning. So he is taking the word on the one hand of a cunning devious bitch. And on the other, of a maniac."

But, as Topping had said, *"they don't know what I know."*

He was still up there, with his trowel.

THE man sitting opposite me in the Steel Works Tavern could remember the labyrinth of streets that used to be outside with sharp, almost photographic clarity. For he had returned to them in his thoughts every day, every night, for 24 years. Paul Reade, that 15-year-old lad whose sister was swallowed up in the maze, was now 39. He still called Pauline 'Our Kid', because to him she would always be young and pretty and 16.

Paul's life, for a reason he found hard to explain, had gone haywire after his sister's disappearance. Eighteen months after she vanished he lost the good, steady job he had had at the upholstery works and within three years he had embarked on a life of petty crime, breaking into shops in the area. He spent two years in Borstal and, coincidentally, his first period of remand was in Risley, near Warrington, in 1966, when two other people were on remand there, facing far more serious charges. Ian Brady and Myra Hindley.

He had married, becoming the father of two daughters, now both in their teens, but his marriage had not worked out and he was now separated.

He now lived in a council house a couple of miles from the house where he, his mother and his father had shared such utter bewilderment and heartache. His mind had reconstructed a thousand times that last walk his sister took in the pale evening sunlight along the rain-dampened pavements on 12 July 1963. He had asked himself a million times *how* Pauline had stepped, that night, into the clutches of evil and *how*, most painfully of all, she had died.

Paul Reade had returned with me to what was left of that area of Gorton now flat and deserted, but haunted by so many ghosts. He could still see the streets brimming with life, hear the chatter in the backyards and the shouts of children at play in the days when Myra Hindley had been the 'big girl' in charge of the games and where Pauline had been blossoming into a beautiful young woman.

He could, I sensed, still feel her presence in that area. He puts his pint glass down on the table and looked at me through the thick lenses of his spectacles. "I don't think our Pauline is on Saddleworth Moor," he said quietly. "I believe she was..." He paused. "I believe she was disposed of a lot closer to home. *Here*, in this area."

I raised my eyebrows. Paul finished his drink. He'd show me what he meant. Outside there was a light drizzle as I followed him along Gorton Lane and past the Vulcan pub. He stopped and pointed up Froxmer Street. "That's where Pauline was last seen," he said. "I believe that half way to the dance at the Railway Institute she changed her mind and turned back, decided she didn't want to go on her own, and in one of those streets she met Myra Hindley and Ian Brady.''

We turned back, skirting the grassed area where the houses of Wiles Street had stood and reached a railway embankment. Paul pointed to his left. "There used to be a fence of railway sleepers there, to stop the kids getting onto the line. I think that after our Pauline was killed her body was lifted over that fence, then carried down the embankment. Follow me.''

We scrambled down the steep slope to the gravelled edge of the track and I followed him for about 200 yards, under a bridge and back up the embankment. A derelict wasteland of rubble met my eyes. He pointed. "This used to be an allotment.'' Then, slowly, he said: ''After our Pauline disappeared a lady who lived nearby said she had seen from her window, late at night – the night she vanished – two people digging here. It was dark. She couldn't make out who they were, two men, two women, a man and a woman, or what, but definitely two people. Digging.''

Who was the lady? Had the police talked to her? Paul shook his head and shrugged. "She's dead now. My dad went to the police about it years ago, but nothing happened.''

Paul had convinced himself, through his countless mental reconstructions of the events on the night his sister went missing, that this now vastly-changed area of Gorton still held the clues. At the time of their arrest, Bannock Street, where Brady had lived with Hindley, had been demolished. Number 7 could have held vital evidence that would have solved the mystery 22 years earlier.

He half closed his eyes to bring back the picture of the corner of Charmers Street where, just before ten o' clock on that dreadful night, he had seen Myra Hindley standing alone. Where was Pauline then? Alive? Dead? The question tortured him.

His mother's life had been ruined. Each episode of the new story that was developing had worsened her physical and mental condition. "In November, after Myra Hindley started to talk to the police, she was taken into hospital with shingles. They let her out for Christmas, but she took bad again on 20 February, two days after our Pauline's fortieth birthday. She is just like a zombie.''

And yet, incredibly, Joan Reade had found forgiveness for Ian Brady and Myra Hindley. Six months earlier she had been interviewed by the Roman Catholic newspaper *The Universe*. She was quoted: "We've got to remember what Our Lord said: 'Father forgive them, for they know not what they do.' We are suffering, but so are Brady and Myra. They are locked in prison for life." It had taken her a long time. "I prayed and prayed until one day I felt it inside me that I really had forgiven," said the tragic mother. Now, Paul told me, following the confession of Myra, she was in a hospital psychiatric ward.

We retraced our steps back to Gorton Lane. Paul blinked at me through the rain. "I want to hear that full statement that Myra Hindley made to the police. Every detail," he said. "There are so many unanswered questions."

I left Paul Reade that afternoon with the questions still tormenting him, still wondering what was going on in the mind of Myra Hindley. Neither of us could know it then, but she had already made her next move in the latest, strange chapter of events.

She had thrown out a challenge to Ian Brady.

★   ★   ★

ON Tuesday, 16 June 1987 Myra Hindley, for the first time, and publicly, turned her contempt on Ian Brady. It was a move calculated to bait and goad her former lover and accomplice, timed to coincide exactly with an unforgettable date on the calendar. The twenty-third anniversary of the disappearance of Keith Bennett.

She knew of the growing criticism of the continuing search on Saddleworth Moor and that the critics were saying "told you so" about the failure of the police to find graves. And that her cooperation, her confession, were being regarded as nothing more than an attempt to win public sympathy for her cause for freedom. Brady's contemptuous silence infuriated her. For all those years he had been winning the bizarre game they had played from their cells. Now she should be winning and he was refusing to play.

So, for the first time in 16 years, she picked up her pen and wrote to him. Not this time the words of love ("*Dearest Ian...you are the only thing that keeps my heart beating, my only reason for living.*") that had once filled her correspondence with him, but now words of bitter frustration. "If you are witholding vital information, for God's sake help those poor families." If he didn't, she said, "the only conclusion is that for your own selfish and morbid gratification you don't ever want this whole ghastly nightmare to end." And: "What difference can it make now to acknowledge those two crimes? We both know we will never be free..."

The contents of the letter were made public on TV, radio and the newspapers. She waited for his reply. And when it came, in a terse statement from his solicitor, her fury, her frustration, grew. "He has not received this letter and he does not wish to receive it," said Mr Birnberg. "If the letter arrives he will instruct the hospital authorities to send it back unopened." And cuttingly: "He regards the whole thing as a public relations stunt."

What Myra did not know was that Brady *had* been talking to the police, though unlike her, he had not publicised the fact. The killer, again without publicity, had been exchanging words with someone else, too.

Ann West.

I HAD shared a secret with Ann West, her husband Alan, and with Ian Brady, for several weeks.

It was over lunch with the couple in a restaurant near Manchester in March that Ann told me they had again started writing to her daughter's murderer. She felt that she might now be able to reach him, touch a nerve by suggesting that Myra Hindley was gloating over the situation in which she had placed him, that she was on an 'ego trip' and that they had not fallen for the con. She might also win his confidence by mentioning that she had met, and liked, his mother. She was not optimistic about getting a response, but she had urged him once more to end the agony of Joan Reade and Winnie Johnson.

The days dragged into weeks. Still no reply. Ann and Alan West shrugged. They had really expected no more. It had been worth trying, even though writing to the man, the monster, in polite terms had gone gratingly against the grain.

And then, at the end of May, I was talking to Alan West on the 'phone. He lowered his voice. "*We've had a letter from Ian Brady*." But please, he said, not a word. They'd made a breakthrough and they didn't want him to dry up on them. I promised to keep the information to myself. It was difficult, as a newspaperman, to share such a secret, but I knew he was right. One whiff of publicity and Ian Brady would not write to them again.

The letter, from Patient No. 490, at Park Lane Hospital, Liverpool, dated 27 May 1987, was only really an acknowledgement. "Dear Mrs West, I received your last letter but decided that I'd reply at a future date when anything definite occurred." But he *had* responded. The mental block had lifted a little.

Ann had not been well. The compulsion that drove her to oppose every move of Myra Hindley also drained her physically. Their next letter to Brady was only two pages long, Alan explaining her illness and adding that cooperation from him – perhaps allowing her to visit him or telling where the missing children were – might help her recover. Was there, they wondered, any scrap of sympathy, any compassion in the twisted, demented mind of Lesley Ann's murderer? Certainly, 23 years ago, he had shown none to *her*. They knew, though, that they had one powerful emotion in common with him. A loathing for Myra.

And on Saturday, 20 June 1987 Ian Brady put pen to paper again. Four days after the goading challenge from Myra Hindley.

"Dear Mrs West, Many thanks for your last letter. The reason I have not replied sooner is that many things that are happening must not reach the Press yet. I suppose you've seen or heard that the Home Office, on the strength of my information, are re-opening the case. I can't tell you anything else. You'll see or read about it soon. Sincerely, Ian Brady. PS: I'm glad you got on well with my mother. She knows nothing at all about the moors, etc."

Ann West found it hard to take her eyes off the letter, particularly the sentence: *"You'll see or read about it soon."*

It was to be much, much sooner than she could ever have dreamed. And what she, and the world, were to see and read about would be the most dramatic chapter in the story of the Moors Murders for almost 22 years.

THE valley was bathed in the rare warm sunshine of the first day of July as the white police van passed through Greenfield and began the now familiar ascent of the A635 to Saddleworth Moor. It was the start of just another day in the routine as the eight policemen watched the moorland scenery slip by once more, the soft green meadows giving way to the harsher, barren landscape as they climbed away from the villages. No one gave the vehicle a second glance. It was now as common a sight as the baker's van or the milkman's float going through Greenfield.

The drill at the summit was the same as always. The eight men, each one hand-picked by Peter Topping and not allowed to clock up overtime to keep down costs on the sensitive assignment, climbed from their van, unloaded their assortment of gardening tools – spades, rakes, trowels – and trudged again into the peat.

Up there, the sunshine was hazier and the temperature much, much lower, the chill wind, even in summer, making weatherproof clothing still necessary. There was no one else on the Moor, no sightseers, no reporters, no photographers. The news editors were bored again by Topping's now-tedious wild goose chase. Why the hell didn't he admit defeat and call it a day?

The small team, though, were no longer working in the Shiny Brook area. They had moved to Hollin Brow Knoll, two miles away and close, very close, to the spot where the body of Lesley Ann Downey had been found and where Myra Hindley had taken them.

The gully of Shiny Brook was saturated by the rain of a dreadful summer and Topping had decided to switch his activities to the higher, drier ground of Hollin Brow Knoll. It was the area he had intended to search last, for the policemen of 1965 had fine tooth-combed the knoll and found no other trace of human remains that had been buried only one or two years earlier. If they could find nothing then, what chance would there be now, 22 years later?

At lunchtime that day, Topping had left his men to work on without his supervision, swapped his anorak and blue overalls for a suit and tie and travelled to Liverpool for another meeting with Ian Brady. For there had been another reason, nothing to do with the weather, for the move to Hollin Brow Knoll. Myra Hindley had remembered something. The detective, even later, would not reveal what it was, but it had caused him to change the pattern of his search, a hunt so painstaking that he had even called in archaeologists to assist. It had been, he said later, an apparently insignificant piece of information that would have meant nothing to anyone not closely involved with the moorland investigation. That day, his men were working on that scrap of information.

Ian Brady, meanwhile, seemed far more approachable. The mental block, the inbuilt defence mechanism that had slammed down on his mind in 1965, the barrier seemingly impenetrable against the relentless invasion of policemen ("*we are making inquiries into the whereabouts of...*") had finally lifted, laid his defences bare.

Even his bitter conflict with Myra seemed to have been

forgotten, his will to win weakened. And it had been brought about by something that, finally, he believed – despite his earlier doubts – had happened. Something he had craved like a chastised child. The forgiveness of the mother of little Lesley Ann Downey.

Of course, Ann West could never forgive him, but by the tone of her letters I believe that Brady had found a comfort. She had found a tiny segment of a mind twisted by evil that, in children, good or bad, only a mother can reach. And the link with Lesley Ann's mother and *his* mother had brought a warmth, almost in the way a child is warmed by a maternal pardon for a wrongdoing he had thought unforgiveable. There was the smugness, too, that a child feels when his wickedness is blamed on a bad playmate.

Conversation was now easier between Brady and Topping. The killer had responded to the gentle, pursuasive tone of the detective who, forever patient, was prepared to sit out the long silences as the man whose mind he was searching helped him to look into its darkest recesses. He knew that he should not push for answers, but wait. *Could Ian remember*…There was an interruption. A telephone call for Mr Topping. The CID chief stood up and stretched, glad, perhaps of the slight diversion, having spent four hours with Brady.

It was a diversion that, in fact, turned out to be anything but slight. For the call, put through to that extension at Park Lane Hospital, was a message from his men on Saddleworth Moor.

Topping nodded, his face giving away nothing as he listened. *He was on his way*. His men *would* be working overtime tonight. He put down the telephone and looked at Ian Brady. There had been a discovery at Hollin Brow Knoll.

A grave.

IT had been mid-afternoon on the knoll. The policemen straightened their backs wearily. Two parts of the day

145

gone, another day, another zero. All day, like all spring, all summer, they had followed the procedure laid down by Topping – digging, trowelling, sifting every grain of peat. They had become so accustomed to finding nothing that their original, natural trepidation towards some dreadful discovery that might haunt them for the rest of their lives had virtually disappeared. Now it was just a day-in, day-out routine. Each spadeful of peat was getting heavier.

They were 150 yards from the road and a little over the same distance from the place where the grave of Lesley Ann Downey had been found, just over the ridge, hidden from the A635. The spades sliced into the squelching black earth, so heavy and clinging that it almost tore their boots from their feet when they struggled through the morass. The top layer was scooped off, the layer beneath carefully examined by trowel. Then again, and again, and again. Nothing. Nothing. Nothing. Almost time to get the flasks out for a cuppa. And then: *Hello, what's this?* There was something, just below the surface, other than the things they were used to finding like rocks or the bones of sheep. They gently scraped away the soaking peat, their hearts pounding, their throats suddenly, painfully, dry. *Oh, God.* It had once been white, was now soiled and faded by weather and time, but it was still being worn. A girl's stiletto-heeled shoe.

At 2.45p.m. on Wednesday, 1 July 1987, his men knew, and soon the world would know, that Peter Topping had been right.

The girl was still wearing the pink dress, the blue coat, the lavender cardigan, the gold-coloured necklace, soiled by the peat, faded by time. Such a long, long time.

Eighteeen miles from a Manchester backstreet, 23 years, 11 months and 20 days after she put on those clothes to go to a dance – and 8755 nightmares later for her mother – they had found Pauline Reade.

THE scene on Saddlworth Moor that summer evening

was reminiscent of two scenes from the same tragedy that had been played out in the October of 1965, when the Moor had yielded two of its dark secrets, the bodies of Lesley Ann Downey and John Kilbride. More police officers arrived, then pathologists, then arc lights and a tent.

The grave, at its shallowist, was only nine inches deep. Her other shoe had been lying on top of her body, which was on its left side, one arm at the side, the other across her shoulder, her legs bent almost double. Delicately, skilfully, Home Office pathologist Dr Geoffrey Garrett and his colleague Dr Michael Green supervised the heart-rending exhumation of Pauline Reade. And then a stretcher and black plastic sheeting were brought to hide the tragic discovery as it was carried by four stumbling, white faced policemen to a waiting, windowless van at the roadside.

The remains were taken to the public mortuary in Oldham, ten miles away. A grim task lay ahead for the pathologists. And for Peter Topping there was a task that night that every policeman in the world dreads: informing the next of kin of a fatality. He had achieved what he had set out to do in finding Pauline (*"I owe it to the families of the missing children"*), and this was the moment he had waited for, but a job he approached with a turmoil of mixed feelings, the reporting of a death almost 24 years after it had happened, to a family who knew it had happened and had wanted this confirmation, but would be none the less devastated.

No job for a rookie – usually the messenger of grim news – this. Topping had led from the front every inch of the way since he first blew the dust from the files of the missing children. He had sped back to Saddleworth Moor as soon as the news had reached him and taken command of the operation with the outwardly brisk detachment of a superbly professional policeman and the inwardly sympathetic sadness of a man who is also a father.

A father faced a father on the doorstep of a council house in a Manchester cul-de-sac that night. On a warm July night, like the July night when one had been plodding the beat as a young bobby, the other settling down to a sleep from which he would awake to a 24-year nightmare. Amos Reade knew why he had come. "Please leave this family alone and in peace," said Peter Topping as he left a father breaking his heart. And wondering how to tell his wife.

Joan Reade, they said, knew nothing. Not even that Myra Hindley had publicly searched her soul and confessed to her involvement "*in these awful events*." Newspapers had been kept from her, she had been shielded from television news reports. Even when her family had tried, when they felt she was having a good day, to gently make her aware of events, their words, said Paul, seemed to go straight through her, failing to register in her tortured, pain-deadened mind. How *could* they tell her that Pauline was no longer a missing person and now a victim of murder?

Officially the body they had found on the Moor was still that of a 'person unknown', and Topping had told Amos Reade he would probably have to talk to him again once further enquiries had been made. He had been preparing him for an ordeal that lay ahead. Identification.

The pathologists found the teenage girl's body to be in a remarkable state of preservation, mummified by the peat, providing horrifying evidence of how she had died. She had received a blow to her forehead, delivered by either a fist or a blunt instrument. But the dreadful injury which took her young life was the larger of two wounds on her neck – a four-inch gash to her throat, inflicted with such force that it had broken the vertebrae at the top of her spinal column.

When that terrible fact emerged, it was obvious what Peter Topping and his men had been seeking on Saddleworth Moor with metal detectors.

A very large knife.

THE sun was shining brightly on Saddleworth Moor the next morning. The anger, the spite, had gone from the weather for the first time, it seemed, in almost a quarter of a century. The sunshine lit the Moor, bathed it in a warmth as if some terrible evil, or at least part of it, had been purged, cleansed.

I had driven up there that day, along, once more, with scores of Pressmen and TV cameraman and we had plodded – many of us in totally unsuitable footwear – through the boggy ground to a square, white plastic tent, behind the walls of which lay a shallow grave, now empty. We blinked in the sunlight as the slim figure in the blue boiler suit walked towards us. Peter Topping, the man who had turned the other cheek to the critics and persevered, dug with spade, trowel, his bare hands, through all the seasons. He faced the Press, not to gloat or say "I told you so" but, his face now relieved of some of the strain, to tell the world: "It's been a team effort.

"You see us up here on a fine day, but I have a small squad of officers and we have endured terrible weather conditions, not just for weeks but for months. Had we unfortunately not found anything up here I would, quite properly, have been asked to justify my actions – and I could have done. There have been a number of reasons why we continued this investigation: the interests of justice, the families and the public. Finding the body brings some peace to the family of the victim. But it is a day when you have got to have mixed feelings. We are pleased and relieved but also realise the dramatic effects on the people concerned."

Myra Hindley, it was said, had wept in her cell when she had been given the news and had been "immensely relieved" that the "whole ghastly episode was coming to an end." But it was not. Topping would go on searching. There was still another child to be found. "It could involve weeks of searching. It is something we have to do," said the policeman, still remembering the sad, anxious face of Winnie Johnson from a visit to her home last night. Yes, he would be back tomorrow with his men. And, though he kept the chilling fact to himself, with someone else by his side.

Ian Brady.

Chapter Thirteen

IN MYRA'S FOOTSTEPS

SLOWLY, in the east, over the 1600 foot ridge, the sun rose, growing bigger, brighter, causing the grey eyes, unaccustomed to its naked light, to blink defensively and the thin hand to reach into an inside pocket for a pair of dark glasses.

The man had been locked up for 7934 days. It was the first sunrise he had seen or felt warm his pale face since he was a young man and *she* had been by his side. And it had risen on a much different world than the one he had left behind on the morning of 7 October 1965 when his freedom ended.

The first event, and the one that affected him most personally, happened *after* his arrest, but *before* his trial – the abolition of hanging for murderers – enabling him, from behind bars, to spectate on history, on scientific achievement, innovation: colour television, the QE2, heart transplants, the outbreak of 'The Troubles' in Northern Ireland, Concorde, the first men landing on the moon, decimalisation, commercial radio, the Common Market, North Sea oil, test tube babies, the first British woman Prime Minister, the Falklands War, breakfast TV, video, Star Wars, Ethiopia, the finding of the Titantic, the Chernobyl nuclear disaster, AIDS...

The man had changed much, too. The last time he had been in this place he had been a strapping, strong 27-year-old. Handsome, arrogant, in command, picnicking, drinking wine, taking photographs. And burying the bodies of children. He was now thinner, more stooping, his hair greyer and the eyes, behind the dark glasses, were haunted with the now vivid memory of that place in which he stood.

Th sun was now climbing in the sky, warming the backs of the men who walked with him, making them loosen their clothing. But he, despite the brightness that hurt his eyes, was cold, so cold. His overcoat remained buttoned, its collar turned up. It was a long, black coat, perhaps the same one he had worn as a young man in the backstreets of Manchester, that had earned him a nickname from his neighbours. They had laughed then, not realising the tragic prophesy of the title they had given him. The Undertaker.

And now that same young man, 22 years older. Ian Brady, was back in the place he had made his own private cemetery.

★   ★   ★

IT had been 3 am when they came for him. It was still dark outside, the hospital in silence as the headlights of the police cars pierced the gloom, sending shadows darting across the grounds of Park Lane. Patient 490 had not slept. There was too much, too many memories, too many ghosts, on his mind. Before him lay perhaps the most unbelievable journey of his life, an excursion into his past – a past that part of him had tried to forget. Yet the prospect of returning to Saddleworth Moor gripped him with the same fearful excitement that had seized Myra Hindley seven months earlier. It was a return to his youth, to the mid-1960s, an escape for a day.

Peter Topping was punctual to the minute. And a few minutes later a convoy of three unmarked cars swept through the gates of the hospital and headed for the M62, the motorway that stretched, straddling the Pennines, from the Mersey to the Humber. Brady was in the middle of the three cars. As with Myra Hindley, they were taking no chances. And the 30 officers 60 miles away, waiting for them, were armed. Douglas Hurd, who had signed the temporary release papers only the day before had insisted there was to be no lapse in security. Ian Brady must be guarded against revenge attacks.

The unfamiliar motorway with its blue and white illuminated signs, like Burtonwood Services (*Burtonwood?*

Didn't that used to be a Yank airforce base?), was soon behind them. They followed the signs to Oldham and, as dawn was beginning to break, to Greenfield and the A635.

Brady peered through the car window as the shapes flitted by, the tumbledown stone walls by the roadside, the deep valley on their right, the landscape on their left rising as they climbed. His heart was beating quickly as it had when he had been Myra's passenger and they had been carrying one of their dreadful secrets. *Keith Bennett.* He could not shut the name from his mind. That was who they were looking for, the little lad with the bad eyesight who never got to his gran's on a summer night 23 years ago. Now only Ian Brady could tell them where his eventual, final destination had been.

It was becoming lighter. Half past four. And on their left, silhouetted against the dawn sky, becoming larger, rising from the ground was a sight that jolted his memory violently, with the severity of an electric shock: the rocks on Hollin Brow Knoll, the silent witnesses to the evil of his youth when he had feverishly dug into the winter-hardened peat to conceal the pitiful remains of a little girl who had begged him for her life.

The police cars slowed as they rounded the bend, then stopped, just past the rocks. Brady shivered, despite the thick overcoat, and nodded slowly, murmuring to himself. Another girl, older than Lesley Ann, before her. Another nod of confirmation. *Pauline Reade.*

Now, where was Keith Bennett? The cars moved off again, along the plateau, the sky brightening, turning bluer as the sun rose to herald a rare, glorious summer day as the vehicles picked up speed along the A635. Curiously, the section along which they were taking the Scotsman was named locally, the Isle of Skye. They travelled for two miles before stopping again, this time overlooking the deep gullies and reservoirs of Wessenden Head Moor and Shiny Brook where Myra Hindley had taken them twice, but had been unable to pinpoint a precise location.

The car door was opened. Ian Brady was helped from

the vehicle. He pushed his hand into his inside pocket and brought out the dark glasses as the light stung his eyes. He looked across the valley and drew in his breath. It was a moment he had never believed would come into his life. Standing *here* again, as though he were free, savouring the air of the moors, the same moors that had not changed, as though 1965 was yesterday and he was 27 again. *Christ, it was beautiful.*

Topping was at his elbow. He pointed across the valley. That's where Myra had taken them. The party of policemen and their new guide still wearing his thick, black overcoat in spite of the rising temperature – a garb that belonged to the 1960s – stepped onto the moorland. In the footsteps of Myra Hindley.

The pale, coarse grass felt springy beneath his feet. He stumbled and almost fell. A policeman's arm helped him regain his balance. The killer, unmanacled for practical purposes, plodded on, deeper into the gully of Shiny Brook, the ground now becoming wet, clinging. Brady glanced over his shoulder, back to the road, now a distant, twisting ribbon. His brow furrowed. The landscape was not exactly as he remembered it. The quarrymen who had been at work since he was last there had altered its features.

OK, said Topping, they'd have a rest, take stock of their surroundings, let Brady gather his thoughts, his recollections. Up above them lay the narrower road to Meltham and there, with camera lenses flashing in the sun's rays, was the Press. Dozens of reporters and photographers, like a faraway grandstand of spectators gathered for a one-man show, stage-managed by Peter Topping, but starring Ian Brady who had had, and perhaps still possessed, so much vanity. A chorus of Nikons screeched from the gallery.

I was among the journalists on the roadside as cameramen trained their telephoto lenses on the strange scene, trying to bring into focus the Moors Murderer and his nine-man escort. Overhead, helicopter flights from a field next to the Huntsman pub on the outskirts of

Holmfirth, was ferrying photographers at £370 an hour. The officers closed in on their charge to try to prevent them taking pictures.

The sun climbed higher. A ring of policemen prevented anyone leaving the road. The search party was now so far away it could not be seen with the naked eye. The cameramen picked out the tiny specks of nine figures with their telephoto lenses and reckoned they must be at least a mile away and a mile from where the grave of the teenage girl had been found two days ago.

We pondered on that. Had a dead child been *carried* all that way, across that terrain where unhampered walkers so often lost their footing? Then I remembered what David Smith had once said to me, in one of our long discussions about the case. He had pondered every possibility of the evil methods of Brady for two decades and had put his suspicions to the police. I recalled his words after he had told me that the police, long ago, had dismissed his suggestion of one possible location of a grave, in Derbyshire, because it was too far from the road to carry a body. "What's wrong with a body *walking* there?" Smith had asked me.

The thought brought a chill to the hot July day, posed a terrible question. Did that little lad who vanished on a summer night in 1964, and for whom they were now looking, fit into that theory? Had Keith Bennett, trusting the grown-ups – it would have been extremely difficult to have taken along an unwilling, struggling child – been alive on that Moor? My suspicions were later confirmed.

Keith Bennett had *walked* to his grave.

★   ★   ★

THAT day, as Ian Brady walked in his past, the police confirmed that the body they had found on Wednesday *was* that of Pauline Reade. Paul sat by his mother's hospital bedside and gazed at the woman whose health had deteriorated so badly that she was not always able to feed herself, and who lay for hours in silence. Doctors had already gently told her about her daughter but, said Paul later, she had not really seemed to understand the terrible news. Her mind, numbed with 24 years of pain, seemed finally deadened, unable to take it in.

Paul Reade himself had been deeply shocked by the discovery. He knew his sister had been murdered and her body concealed, but he had not believed that her remains had been on Saddleworth Moor. As he had told me less than three weeks earlier he had thought she had been "disposed of a lot closer to home."

He did not know it yet, but the subsequent findings of the pathologists, the police and the coroner, pointed to the near-certainty that the knife that slashed Pauline's throat and took her life had been wielded on Saddleworth Moor; that she had been taken there, lured there, walked through the peat and then murdered in the spot where she was buried. There was little doubt, they believed, that she had been coaxed to *his* place, *their* place, instead of going to the dance for the first, and last, time. *"Fancy a run out, Pauline...?"*

We were to learn, much later, that the collar of Pauline's coat and her gold-coloured necklace had been forced into the dreadful wound, presumably in an attempt to stem the heavy bleeding that would have resulted.

There were still many unanswered questions for Paul Reade. How *did* Pauline get to Saddleworth Moor? How was she coaxed there, from the backstreets of Gorton? If only he could have read the mind of Myra Hindley, standing on that street corner on the night of 12 July 1963.

What of the two people, seen digging on the allotment? Was that just hearsay, the colourful imagination of a Gorton caught up in the mystery and evil of the deeds of two of its former residents?

Or *was* someone hiding something that night? The police have never found the murder weapon.

IAN BRADY sank down on a rock and opened the packet of sandwiches, made in the police station canteen and handed to him by a policeman. The last time he had eaten sandwiches there Myra had made them and they had been washed down with wine from the off licence in Gorton or Hyde. Peter Topping was his companion now. They sat together in the sunshine, the murderer and the policeman. It was a strange picnic, so unlike the picnics he had shared with her. They had been a break from hiding a body; this a break from trying to find one.

The thought of death had not been far from Brady's mind for a quarter of a century. He had thought much of his own, doubtlessly of how his life might have ended with the hangman's rope when he was 27 or by the gun of an avenging relative of one of his victims, perhaps *today*. He looked around him. Miles and miles of emptiness. Not a soul. Just him and the nine policemen. And, somewhere, a dead boy.

He had thought, often, about taking his own life and it had been reported that he had said he would, once he had confessed all. It was also said that stripped electrical wiring and a twisted metal coat hanger, as if the instruments of suicide by electrocution, had been found in his hospital room at Park Lane two months ago. But, it was said sceptically, he had deliberately planted the equipment to make doctors think his mental condition was worse than they believed. The last thing he wanted was to be considered sane enough to be returned to prison.

There was little doubt that Brady was severely disturbed mentally, but it suited his purpose to be considered mad. The accommodation in which he spent his life was vastly superior to that inside a jail. And his 'madness' was a barrier behind which he could hide, perhaps providing a reason for his crimes, suggesting he had always had that streak of insanity. It was easy to see how this had infuriated Myra, who had scoffed that her former lover was not mad. For if he was considered so in the eyes of the world, she would compare unfavourably with him. She had no excuse. *She* was responsible for *her* actions. She was *sane*.

Brady looked again at the vast wilderness around him and up at the immense blue sky. This was freedom. The greatest gift to man, next to life. He could feel it, taste it. The coldness was gone from his body. He rose to his feet, peeled off the black overcoat. *Ready?* The ten men moved off again across the Moor.

He stumbled down hillsides, dragged his feet through the quagmire of rain-soaked peat, stopping often to take account of his surroundings. Was it this way, that way? It had been a long, long, time, 23 summers.

That day Ian Brady covered five miles with the patient Topping by his side. He was exhausted, yet at the same time, invigorated by the experience of the sun, the sky, liberty, and the starring role. He spent ten hours on the Moor. It had been an event in criminal history. And, strangely, while he had been there, another chapter of history had been written about another evil man. As Brady sampled freedom, Klaus Barbie, the man they called the Butcher of Lyon, one of the Nazis he had admired so much, a man who deported hundreds of Jews and Resistance workers to their deaths, who sent little children to the hell-hole of Auschwitz, was locked up for life in France, 42 years after the war.

Brady, Topping and the eight other men slowly retraced their path across the Moor, the killer being transported the last few hundred yards to the main road along the rough, unmade track to the reservoirs by Range Rover, a blanket covering his head. They had found nothing, though his solicitor said later: "Mr Topping informed me that he is entirely satisfied that Mr Brady tried his utmost. He gave his all, physically and mentally, in the task." And the CID chief said there was one site he wanted to search more thoroughly, though he needed at least two weeks of good weather to dry out the area before he could begin.

In the police car Ian Brady looked over his shoulder as the hills, the ravines, the rocks, were left behind. His taste of freedom was over. The Moor still held his secret, guarded it so closely, it seemed, that even he could not find it. It appeared that he had failed. But *had* he?

For one fact remained as he descended Saddleworth Moor to go back to the confines of a mental hospital. If a grave had been found, that would have been that. Myra had been back twice. She had begged to stay. For once, in many, many years he knew what she meant, they had one thing in common. And, like Myra, he had told them he wanted to go back...

The Devil's Disciple had fallen again under the spell of Saddleworth Moor.

★   ★   ★

THE following Monday morning, Peter Topping had another man by his side on the moors – the Chief Constable of Greater Manchester, James Anderton. His visit was a public recognition of the work of the detective who had justified his backing, despite all the criticism about wasted police time, manpower and money. The bearded police chief, shirt-sleeved in the continuing heatwave joined his boiler-suited head of CID in the area where Ian Brady had trod three days earlier, and declared: "I have come here to congratulate my officers on their outstanding success and achievements against all the odds. Mr Topping has done a tremendous job under enormous pressure and at times tremendous hostility. I would hope this operation will lead to the final story being told – the book being closed on one of the most horrendous series of crimes against children ever told."

The quiet man in the boiler suit by now knew the whole story, or at least the gospel of evil as told by Myra Hindley. Her words, the previous February, had been tape-recorded by the policeman. But he could not close the book yet. Keith Bennett was still missing and his mother's agony had increased with the realisation that her little lad could have met his dreadful fate in *that* terribly desolate place.

He said, as much for the benefit of Winnie Johnson as for the Pressmen: "We've got an area to be searched and we know what we are looking for. We've got to pinpoint the area where we hope to find the grave of Keith

Bennett.'' He shrugged. "There have been some changes in the landscape and, of course, it's been a long time since *he* has been up here. Please don't get at me if something doesn't happen today, tomorrow or the day after.''

Topping had come so far. In a few months he had closed a 24-year gap of mystery, unlocked secrets from the minds of Ian Brady and Myra Hindley. One secret remained. The whereabouts of Keith Bennett. *They,* apparently, couldn't remember and the only other holder of the secret, Shiny Brook, wasn't telling.

The haunted David Smith had by this time been drawn back into the story. Geoffrey Dickens MP, without naming names, had said that a 'Third Man' may have been involved in the crimes. He was prepared to steer the police towards his sources of information. Smith, though he had not been named, defended himself publicly, challenging the MP to name him in public. The law, 22 years earlier, had cleared him of any involvement, despite the attempts of Brady and Myra to implicate him when they stood trial.

Surprisingly, it was Myra Hindley herself who swung the spotlight away from the 'Third Man'. Her solicitor announced that she had told him there was no third person involved in the killings of four of the victims. "If, however, he (Mr Dickens) is referring to the killing of Edward Evans, then there was a third man involved and my client has given full details of that to the police,'' he said. (Smith, as I explained in an earlier chapter, had been present as Ian Brady dealt the final death blows, with an axe, to Edward Evans. Brady had claimed, in his first statement to the police following his arrest, that Smith had hit Edward Evans with a stick and kicked him.)

Now Myra was putting the spotlight fully on herself. Her solicitor repeated that she knew, by her revelations, that she could be putting herself back in the dock. The last time she was in the dock, she now realised, 22 years too late, she had played it all wrong. The calmness, the lack of emotion, the lack of remorse. The game of Ian Brady. If only she had a second chance to state her case. (*"He*

*became my God, my idol, my object of worship. He could
have told me that the earth was flat, that the moon was
made of green cheese, that the sun rose in the west and I
would have believed him. Such were the powers of his
persuasion.''*) Why hadn't she said that then? The Trilby
to his Svengali?

Did Myra Hindley, I wondered, *want* to be put back on
trial?

THE anguish of Mrs Johnson was probably worse than
ever as the mental picture of her little son, alone, terribly
afraid on that Moor, finally meeting his death where no
one could hear the cries that were finally silenced with
death, plagued her. She had hidden her anger for many
years, but now she said: "If I could have got my hands on
Brady and Hindley I would have torn them apart." And
the bitterness of the families increased with a report that
Lord Longford had once more mentioned the question of
freedom for Myra Hindley. He was not, it was said,
suggesting her release just *now*, while the search was going
on, but he felt that ultimately she should be paroled. In
fairness, he said, the question had been put to him. But,
said his critics, he should have kept quiet. Particularly
now.

It was a wretchedly distressing time for the Reade
family. Amos Reade had been shown the pink party dress
he had last seen his daughter wear 24 years ago. And the
white shoes and the gold-coloured necklace, just as on
those dreadful days in the autumn of 1965, Sheila Kilbride
had identified a check-pattern jacket and Ann West had
been shown a red and green tartan skirt and a little string
of white beads. Like them, he had nodded numbly, the
tears welling in his eyes. Yes, they were Pauline's.

The inquest on Pauline was opened at Oldham, ten miles
from where her body had been found. Mr Reade, now 62,
listened silently, his head bowed, as Detective Chief
Superintendent Topping told how they had found Pauline

and confirmed that he believed her death was the result of a criminal act. The coroner, Mr Bryan North, adjourned the hearing, provisionally for two months, saying: "Within that period I hope that certain decisions will be made as to whether or not prosecutions will be made against any person or persons and if any further inquest is to be carried out."

Meanwhile Ian Brady was longing for a second chance to go back to the moors. Within days of returning to his room at Park Lane he twice appealed to the police to allow him to go there again with Topping. In mid-July he had even made a plea through his usual 'post office', the BBC, saying he was "frustrated", and adding: "I want a second chance to study the area in question."

Why was he being ignored? He had had long, long talks with Topping, told him so much. Why wouldn't they take him back to the Moor? The gullies, the rocks, the ravines, the freedom...His frustration grew. What could he do? And then, his eyes narrowed. A plan began to form in his mind, a mind still dwelling in the 1960s. He would use *her* method. Publicity. He picked up his pen.

On Tuesday, 4 August 1987 another letter arrived at the BBC in London. And the next morning the headlines screamed.

BRADY: FIVE MORE KILLINGS.

Chapter Fourteen

THE "HAPPENINGS"

IN 1965, following the arrest of Ian Brady and Myra Hindley, rumour had been rife as to the extent of the Moors Murderers' activities. As a young reporter with the *Manchester Evening News*, covering the case for my paper, I had heard speculation that Ian Brady had claimed many more victims than the three for whom he stood trial and the two youngsters for whom the police were still then searching.

The files on every missing person and every unsolved murder in Manchester were brought out and police in Glasgow, where Brady had lived until he was almost 17 and had since visited, combed through their 'missing persons' records. But the long passage of time dimmed the possibility of further atrocities from public memory. Until now.

Twenty-two years after all the speculation, I was on holiday in Cornwall with my wife and two teenage daughters when, early one evening, the 'phone in the hotel room buzzed. It was Jeff McGowan, my news editor. Ian Brady had written to the BBC about *five* more murders. What did I think? Could it be possible? Who could the victims be?

Curiously, Brady had referred to the five killings as 'happenings'. Never once, in his letter, did he use the word murder. He began, tellingly, with his recollection of his visit to the Moor: "Yes, it was weird seeing the place again, all that space and vastness. But when we reached the slope where Keith Bennett was, I couldn't find the ravine. We searched from early morning till late afternoon, and I wanted to continue, but a police convoy picked us up. I kept repeating to Mr Topping that I needed a second chance at it, but without any success."

He continued: "I've also given Mr Topping details of

happenings, but he doesn't seem interested in them, i.e. a man on a piece of waste ground near Piccadilly, a woman in a canal, a man in Glasgow, and another on the slopes of Loch Long etc (the latter two were shot at close range. So that's how things stand at the moment." And then:

"There's another on the opposite side of the moor road, one had a rag tied on the wooden post as a marker, but, unknown to me, all the wooden posts had been changed to plastic."

Five "*happenings...*" It was as if Ian Brady could not bring himself to use the words 'murders' or 'killings' or 'deaths', as if the mental block rejected them. What could those "happenings" have been?

He had written of "*a man on a piece of waste ground near Piccadilly*". One case seemed to fit that location. In the early 1960s the body of a railway worker was found on waste land near Manchester's Piccadilly station. His murderer was never caught.

"*A woman in a canal*". There were, so far as the police were concerned, no unexplained canal deaths at that time. And to drag every inch of the miles and miles of canal in Greater Manchester was not an operation that would even be considered. Names of women who were murdered in the area in the early 1960s were mentioned in the Press, but none of the cases really seemed to fit.

"*A man in Glasgow and another on the slopes of Loch Long (shot at close range)*". Brady had been born in Glasgow and lived there until he was almost 17. And, during the late summer of the year they were arrested he and Myra had spent a holiday in Scotland. He certainly had the means of shooting someone – a Webley '45 and a Smith and Wesson '38. The hand guns were bought for him, as he had asked, by Myra, who had joined a rifle club, also at his wish. He regularly carried the Smith and Wesson in a shoulder holster.

The police dug out all the files once again. If Brady was to be believed he had been killing adults as well as children all those years ago. It *was* possible for, soon before his arrest, he had confessed to David Smith that he preferred his victims to be between the ages of 16 and 21 because the police did not pay all that much attention when people in that age bracket went missing.

"Another one on the opposite side of the Moor road". If that, too, were true, then the victim was most unlikely to be a child, simply because there were no other unclosed files on missing children from the days when Brady had been at large in Manchester. Who, then? A tramp, an itinerant picked up on the A635 in the city, someone who would not be reported missing? Someone from another town, another city many miles away? The possibilities, the permutations, were endless.

Topping already knew of Brady's claim and said that obviously he would carry out a full investigation. Detectives from Glasgow travelled to Manchester to confer with him. They could not ignore the claimed "happenings." Myra Hindley said she had no knowledge of other killings, but she had told the police chief not to discount her former lover's words. Her solicitor said: "It was our feeling that it is unlikely Brady would be fabricating any of these events. We all said it could not be assumed that he has been fantasizing just because he is a mental patient."

The mental patient had got his publicity. Would *that* get him back to Saddleworth Moor?

★　　★　　★

SO, very slowly, little faster than she would have clicked along there in her white high heels, Pauline Reade went once more along Gorton Lane, on Friday, 7 August 1987; along the road she had last travelled alive on another Friday, 24 years, three weeks and five days ago. She was back in the place where she had skipped and played as a little girl, hoped and dreamed as a teenager and, at the dawn of her womanhood, walked to her death.

As on the last time, she was going to her grave, but on this occasion to a final, blessed resting place.

The people of Gorton – a Gorton she would not have

recognised, stripped of so many of its streets, terraces and backyards – stood at their doors in silence as, in the rain, Pauline came home. Not from the dance, but from a lonely unhallowed tomb high above the city, in which, for all those years, she had worn her dance dress. Some of those, young wives, mothers, would not have been born when she last passed by. But they cried, just the same, as the girl who would by now have been middle-aged, perhaps with children of her own, even looking forward to the prospect of being a grandmother, made her last journey in this world in a hearse.

Joan Reade, dressed in black, a poor, bewildered, sick woman, thin through the long years of torture, her hair, which would now be white, dyed black, was there to say 'Goodbye', instead of the casual 'tarrah' with which they had last parted. This time she would know where her daughter was going. Husband Amos and son Paul supported the frail woman, who had been allowed from her psychiatric ward with three nurses to attend her. It was a day they had long awaited, to give 'Our Pauline' a decent, Christian burial, yet it was a dreadful ordeal.

The funeral service was at the church of St Francis, whose school she had attended and where, with her devout Catholic mother, she had gone to Mass. Peter Topping was there, with his team, now in dark suits and black ties, to pay their respects. A card on their wreath said: "With deepest sympathy. From the Moors enquiry team." Others who understood the deep hurt were there. Ann West, Winnie Johnson and Patrick Kilbride. They too sent flowers and cards.

Joan Reade, standing later at Gorton Cemetery, swaying between her husband and son, watched as the light oak coffin was gently lowered into the ground, its plaque simple, matter of fact. *"Pauline Reade. Died 12th July 1963. Aged 16 years."* It was an almost mechanical motion as, in the tradition of a Christian burial, she dropped a thin handful of wet, but homely, Manchester soil into the grave that would be adorned with their wreaths of chrysanthemums and roses, their cards: "Rest in peace, now Pauline.

Your loving parents, Joan and Amos'' and ''Pauline. I love you so much. Your brother Paul. God bless.''

There was a card, too, from Pat Cummings, who should have gone to the dance with Pauline, but instead went to the cinema. ''Pauline. No words can express how I feel at this moment.'' The sentiment described also the hidden turmoil of the three people, the mother, the father, the brother, standing mutely at that graveside, the rain mingling with the tears on their faces. *Welcome* Pauline. *Goodbye* Pauline.

Gently, they took Joan Reade back to hospital.

THE guards at Cookham Wood prison were now keeping a close watch on Myra Hindley. There were those 'legit' prisoners, who – whatever the 'remorse,' however long ago the crimes – held no brief for the molesters and killers of children. Now, sickened by the full horror of the Moors Murders story, a new generation of inmates, some of them mothers themselves, was out to get her. Twice, in the first week of August it was reported that she was attacked while her 'minders' ' backs were turned.

For Myra, despite the niche she had carved out for herself, the cocoon of hangers-on who protected her, it was a reminder of those early days in Holloway when one ferocious assault by a girl of 20 left her with a broken nose and a suspected jaw fracture. The injuries had necessitated plastic surgery which had changed her appearance, leading to suspicions, as long ago as 1976, that she was being prepared for eventual release.

There was no doubt that, had Myra's intention been to win public support by her show of remorse and helpfulness to the police and the revelation of a secret she had kept for 24 years, she had succeeded only in hardening the resolve of those who wanted to keep her behind bars. By her words, her actions, and the subsequent discovery, she had made that life behind bars so much more difficult for herself.

If the police, still searching on the moors, found the body of Keith Bennett, the pressures, the dangers, would increase. But Topping and his men, patiently and systematically combing every inch of ground, were getting nowhere. The trouble was that neither of the murderers could remember exactly where the little lad's grave had been dug. Perhaps, it was argued, there might be a result if Brady and Hindley could retrace their damning steps *together*...

The prospect was mind-boggling, for some too bizarre to contemplate, but it was one of the many possibilities being considered by the policemen who knew that without a further lead, a new clue, the task in that immense wilderness was almost hopeless. On Monday 24 August, Peter Topping announced that he had called off the search, saying it would be resumed only if he thought he had new information.

The following day he was again at Cookham Wood, for he now had to complete his file for the Director of Public Prosecutions who would decide whether or not there would be charges laid against Myra and Brady. He spent five hours with her. But when he came away he was still no closer to the grave of Keith Bennett.

Winnie Johnson's thoughts now dwelt almost entirely on the night of Tuesday, 16 June 1964 after she had watched Keith disappear from her sight for the last time. She tried, as a mother would, to put herself by her son's side – if *only* she *had* been – to share his feelings, his final fear, his pain. They were feelings that four other mothers knew all about, though they had graves, with headstones and loving inscriptions to visit and place flowers upon.

Even so there were still many unanswered questions for them. The cause of death of the oldest victim, 17-year-old Edward Evans, was obvious. Fourteen axe wounds in his head, inflicted at 16 Wardle Brook Avenue, where the police had found his body the next day. And then, as though that were not enough, a length of electric cable twisted and tightened around his neck to ensure that his young life had finally expired. In the cases of Lesley Ann

Downey and John Kilbride it had been impossible for the pathologists to ascertain the causes of death. There were no obvious signs of violence on their bodies, but at the trial of Ian Brady and Myra Hindley the prosecution asserted that the method of killing was almost certainly asphyxia. At the time, the Attorney-General Sir Elwyn Jones declared that "the jury might come to the conclusion that asphyxia was at any rate attempted in the case of Edward Evans. The difference there was he may well have died before the strangling ligature was applied to his neck."

The cruel, horrible way in which Pauline Reade – the first known victim – had met her death had been leaked to the Press and as it tore at the hearts of her family, it increased the agony of Mrs Johnson and, inevitably, that of the other mothers. Ann West could not tear her mind from the night of 26 December 1964. She found herself in that bedroom at 16 Wardle Brook Avenue, where her little daughter had begged and pleaded for her life. She *had* to know about Lesley Ann's last hours, minutes, to share them in retrospect with her.

In that late summer of 1987 Mrs West sat down and wrote another letter, this time to the woman she had sworn to kill if ever she walked free, to whom she had devoted her life to hating. *"Miss Hindley"* – she could not bring herself to start with the word 'dear' – *"Many years ago my daughter begged you for her life..."*

Two months passed. Silence. Ann West was not surprised. It was no more than she had expected. What she did not know, however, was that Myra Hindley in her cell at Cookham Wood, was carefully weighing every word, penning a long letter, filling seven pages of blue prison notepaper with an astonishing reply to the mother of the ten-year-old girl whose life she had taken at Christmas.

"DEAR Mrs West, Thank you for your letter, and I'm sorry it has taken me so long to reply to it. I think I know how difficult it must have been to write to me, and this

reply is going to be even more difficult, because I find it almost impossible to express the way I feel about the indescribable suffering I have caused you, your family and the other families concerned."

The letter from Prisoner 964055 dropped through Ann West's letter box in early October. The neat handwriting was almost schoolgirlish, but in the eloquent English of the scholar she had become through her long studies for an Open University Bachelor of Arts degree.

"It is true what you say in your letter about my never having written to you during all these years to express any sorrow or remorse, but I want you to know that in the early 1970s, after having read something about you in the Press, I did ask the authorities in Holloway if I could write to you (rules about correspondence have changed in the last few years) and if I could ask you to visit me, despite your threats to kill me if you ever get the chance. But I was advised against writing, and an adamant refusal was given for a visit to take place. In retrospect, I know the letter I would have written then would not have been as frank as this one, because you must be aware that it has taken me a very long time – much too long – to come to terms with what Ian Brady and I did all those years ago.

"I could not even face the truth myself, let alone tell the truth to anyone else. This is unforgiveable, and I do not expect anyone, especially yourself, to understand the reason for my long silence, and many denials. I know almost everyone describes me as cold and calculating – "evil Myra" – but I ask you to believe that I find this deeply upsetting. I was evil, and I make no excuses whatsoever for my part in any of the past.

"The letter from Mrs Johnson last October absolutely devastated me, and made me realise finally that I could no longer remain silent, whatever the cost to my family or myself. In February this year I gave as full and detailed account as I could to Mr Topping of what happened to your daughter..."

Mrs West caught her breath. It was not easy for her to read on.

"I now want to say to you, and I implore you to believe me, because it is the truth, that your child was not physically tortured, as it is widely believed. I said at my trial, and I say to you now, that my involvement in the events on that tape-recording were indefensible and that I accepted any derogatory adjective used to describe my conduct. But please believe me – not for my sake, but simply in the hope that it will give you even a little peace of mind, that however monstrous and unforgiveable the crime was, your child was not tortured to death."

Ann West shook her head in disbelief. And remembered that tape recording when it was played to her after they had found her little girl's body. She would never forget the cries, the pleading.

However the letter contained a surprising gesture towards David Smith, Myra's former brother-in-law on whom she and Brady had laid a curse before they were jailed for life by implicating him in the death of Lesley Ann. She had claimed that on the night she vanished Smith had taken Lesley Ann to the house in Hattersley and had left with her. The law had believed David Smith but, as he once told me bitterly, a lot of the mud had stuck. She went on with this admission:

"I want to take this opportunity to say that there was no 'third man' involved in your daughter's case. Ian Brady and I lied at our trial about my former brother-in-law's alleged involvement. If this led you to believe he was implicated, as I recollect was the case, then his liberty over the years may have been a source of distress to you. But he didn't have anything to do with it, and I have done him a worse injustice in this respect than he did me by giving false evidence for the Crown about the death of Edward Evans, when in fact he should have been charged and put in the dock with Ian Brady and myself."

That final sentence, though, had carried a sting in its tail for Smith, whom the murderers had alleged had hit and kicked Edward Evans during that terrible scene at 16 Wardle Brook Avenue: a false claim that had been dismissed by the law.

170

"But to return to your letter, you say 'I could never blame your mother for what happened. It wouldn't be right. So I don't expect you to blame me for all the heartache I have had over these years.' Of course it wouldn't be right to blame my mother. She, and Mrs Brady, are, in a different sense, two more innocent victims of Ian Brady's and my perpetrations. My own mother, and my family, have endured terrible sufferings through me, and are still serving, like yourself, an unbearable life sentence. This is yet another burden of guilt I carry, and the weight of it is almost more than I can bear.

"The same is true of the sufferings and heartaches I have caused you and the other families. How can I possibly blame you for the thing I am responsible for? And how can I blame you for the more than understandable hatred you feel for me? I do understand your hatred, of course I do, but believe me Mrs West, you couldn't hate me more than I hate myself. I have asked God for His forgiveness, but I couldn't ask you for yours, for how can I expect you to forgive me when I cannot forgive myself? I have to live with the past for the rest of my life, with self-inflicted wounds to my mind and heart which I doubt will ever heal.

"Having finally and fully acknowledged and confessed these heinous crimes, and realised the dreadful enormity of them, the guilt and the remorse I feel is agonising – the wounds have re-opened and are raw-edged and festering. But I deserve it all, because irrespective of how I became involved in those monstrous crimes at the age of 20, I was a woman, a young one, but still a woman, and an utter disgrace to womankind, as you yourself have said, as have others, and rightly so.

"Mrs West, can I ask you to believe the woman I now am, aged 45, that I am not what I was all those years ago, and to accept that my sincerity is genuine in respect of my deep regret and remorse for all the pain and heartache I have caused you and your family. No words can adequately express what I feel, or what I wish with all my heart you could understand. To say 'I'm truly and deeply

171

sorry' sounds so futile, but I am truly and deeply sorry, and sorry also for taking all these years to say so.

"In the past it seemed an impossible task to write to you when you were quite rightly fighting so hard against my release from prison. There is no need to do that any longer, because I have finally accepted my fate, and know that release from prison is no longer a practical reality. I have written to the Home Office and the Parole Board to say I do not wish to be considered for parole in 1990, and my belief is that I shall remain in prison until I die. So be it. I've brought it all on myself.

"Since my confession to Mr Topping in February this year, the police have been able to find Pauline Reade's body, and her family have been able to give her a Christian burial at last. I am deeply sorry that the case is not yet true for Keith Bennett. I pray and hope with all my heart that the police resume the search, and I promise you, as I'm writing to Mrs Johnson to promise her, that I will continue to do everything possible to help them find her son so that she and her family can be relieved of some of their grief.

"It is true I wanted to send a message to the Reade family, but I was advised against it, as it was feared it would intensify their grief. But Mass was said here for Pauline and her family and I will write to them when I feel they are able to accept a letter from me.

"There is one last thing I would like to say to you. As I wrote above, I do understand your hatred, and I've said that you couldn't hate me more than I hate myself. I know that nothing can change the past, and that you can never forgive or forget the loss of your child, or that any words of mine can bring her back to you. But what I do wish for you, Mrs West, is that eventually your hatred can subside to enable you to gain some measure of peace of mind. I know from my self-hatred that it corrodes the spirit and leads to despair that is unbearable to live with. You've suffered more than enough; please don't add to your suffering by a hatred that I'm not worthy of, and will fester in your heart and mind more than it already has, through my fault.

"This has been a very long letter and will have been painful for you to have read, just as it has been painful for me to have written, knowing that it will have re-opened your own wounds yet again. I want to say to you from my heart, as God is my witness, that my sorrow and remorse for everything is truly genuine, and I hope that you accept it as the truth.

"If you can't bring yourself to believe me – and I have no ulterior motive in writing to you, other than my genuine wish to answer your letter – I will try to understand, and will continue to pray for you, for peace for you, and a healing of your pain and heartache. Yours sincerely, Myra Hindley."

Ann West laid down the letter and looked up at her husband Alan. Her eyes were cold, there was no forgiveness in her heart, one word on her lips.

Liar.

MYRA Hindley was to see that letter, her words, again. On Monday, 12 October it was printed, word for word, in the *Daily Mirror* beneath the gigantic headline 'I AM AN UTTER DISGRACE TO WOMANKIND'. Ann West had decided that the world should see what her daughter's murderer had to say for herself and felt it would come to the same conclusion she had reached without hesitation.

Mrs West told the *Daily Mirror:* "I set a trap for Hindley and this letter proves she's fallen right into it. I've conned her just like she's been conning everyone that she's a changed woman. Now anyone can read this letter and they'll know that there's no way she's a reformed character. She's still as big a monster and as big a liar as she was 23 years ago when my Lesley was murdered. In her letter to me she begs me to believe that my little girl wasn't physically hurt or tortured to death. How can she lie like that? She obviously doesn't know that I heard the tapes and saw the photographs of how my little girl suffered." The letter, she said, had made her hate Myra Hindley even more.

Its sensational publication, it was said, had upset Myra. She had never intended that her letter should be made public. Her solicitor said she had marked it "Confidential; copyright."

The *Daily Mirror* stoutly defended the publication. It was simply not true that the letter had been marked "confidential," it said. "It had the initials PNFP at the top. That, it is now said, meant 'Please not for publication.' Why didn't she spell it out if she really meant it?"

Did she really want her letter kept secret? Did she really believe that such a letter to the woman who had been without doubt, the most strenuous opponent to her cause for freedom, who had used publicity so effectively as a weapon to keep her behind bars, would be kept private? It fostered a belief that Myra Hindley had *wanted* the world to see her words. The letters PNFP – she had used them for many years on the letters she had sent to former jail cronies who had lost no time in running to the newspapers with them – would have meant nothing to Ann West. And she *knew* that Mrs West had, only a few months earlier, released her letter from Ian Brady to the Press. Was Myra's game to play down the dreadful circumstances under which little Lesley Ann Downey died?

But the eyes and ears of Ann West would forever see and hear what took place in that bedroom in Wardle Brook Avenue. The nine photographs of her daughter, naked except for her shoes and socks, a scarf around her mouth. The tape recording, with Myra Hindley's voice: *"Shut up or I'll forget myself and hit you one. I'll hit you one."* And Lesley Ann's: *"Please, God, help me..."*

"She's evil, evil, evil. Always was. Always will be," said Ann West. And to the popular Press she was still Evil Myra.

But what did their readers, the public, think? Was opinion beginning to veer towards Myra Hindley? On Wednesday 14 October *The Star* published the results of a telephone poll from its readers who had been asked, in the light of Myra's letter to Mrs West, for their verdict. The vote of 90 per cent could be summed up in one phrase.

Keep her locked up, and throw away the key.

Chapter Fifteeen

NO FLOWERS FOR KEITH

IN the summer, when she had had hope, Winnie Johnson had stood in her garden in the sunshine and said it was her dearest wish to smother the Christian grave of her son with the roses that surrounded her, in a riot of cheerful colour. But summer had turned to autumn and then to winter. The roses had withered and died. And so, almost, had her hopes. Keith was still buried, on that Moor on the horizon that could be seen from Manchester. But where? *"Please, God, help them to find him,"* she had prayed in church.

She felt so helpless. She knew no man could have done more than Peter Topping to try to end her sadness, to grant her wish that had, just a few months ago, seemed so likely to come true. But the search had been called off. They weren't looking for her little lad any more. They had run out of clues, and had, it seemed, given up. Keith Bennett, Rest In Peace. Wherever you are.

Peter Topping, though, had not given up. Since calling of the search on the Moor he had seen Myra Hindley and Ian Brady a number of times to talk to them and show them video films of the area where they had both searched with him in vain. Now he was searching minds, probing memories.

The sad eyes of Winnie Johnson were the spur, just as the sadness in the eyes of the mothers of missing children had spurred policmen in 1965. But *they* had not had the eager services of the murderers themselves at their disposal. It was a facility that Topping was going to put to the test one more time.

So, on a sharply cold winter's morning, 8 December 1987, he granted Ian Brady *his* dearest wish.

He took him back to Saddleworth Moor.

THE last time he had been there the sun had warmed his face, almost as if in welcome. Today, the Moor, stripped of its sparse summer plumage, now harsh with winter, frowned on the slight figure that had returned to try to wrest the secret it had left within its folds all those seasons ago. The wind from the east whipped his pale face, forcing the colour to his gaunt cheeks.

He had felt the same excitement as five months earlier when, before daybreak, they came to take him from Park Lane, back to being a young man. It made him feel important, wanted, needed. *She* had been there twice, now he was going back for a second time. *Myra: two*; *Ian: two*.

Peter Topping knew everything, from the words that had gushed from Myra Hindley in February, like a torrent whose floodgates had opened. Now the flood had stopped: she could remember no more. The key to unlocking the final mystery was held, it seemed, by Ian Brady, a mental patient who had become disorientated, confused by his surroundings, the last time he had been to the Moor. Brady, though, had begged for another chance. He was more sure this time that he could help. Topping owed it to Winnie Johnson to give him that chance.

The temperature was near freezing as they stepped once more over the ground, now hardened with frost, that led towards Shiny Brook on Wessenden Head Moor. There was just a handful of officers this time. There were no handcuffs on Ian Brady and in place of the almost comical black overcoat, he wore, like most of them, a green anorak and woollen hat. Despite the severe cold, it was a bright day, with the slopes and rocks that might have been landmarks, standing out clearly. Brady glanced around him and nodded towards one of the slopes. The policemen followed the stumbling figure alongside their chief, watched as he stopped, peered at the ground, looked around him, an exercise repeated again and again. They knew, then, in their hearts, that Ian Brady was just as lost as they were. It was an area where they had already covered every inch of thousands of square yards. The sad truth was that he had forgotten. Like a man in the desert he did not know which way to turn.

They spent nine hours at Shiny Brook before Ian Brady, still maintaining that he had taken them to the right spot, was helped into a police van and, with darkness falling, was driven back to Park Lane.

Topping sighed. No, he told reporters later, he had no plans to go back up there.

★   ★   ★

ANOTHER year began. 1988. And on its second day, alone in his mental hospital room, Ian Brady opened his eyes to his fiftieth birthday. Fifty. A time when a man takes stock of his life, asks himself what he has done with it, and wonders if it is too late to put right the mistakes of his earlier years. A time when many questions he asks himself begin with the words *if only*...

There would be many 'if onlys' in his mind. If only he'd stayed in Glasgow. If only he hadn't met *her*. If only he hadn't told David Smith his secrets. If only he were 27 again. And free.

The 'if only' in Peter Topping's mind that New Year was still 'if only we could find Keith Bennett.' He had thought of, and tried, every way to jog memories, particularly those in the clearer mind of Myra Hindley. He had taken her back in her cell, in her mind, many times to Shiny Brook, shown her the videos, the aerial photographs taken by the RAF. Where, Myra, *where*? How could he make her remember. And then the thought had occurred. There was someone who could transport her back there, in her thoughts, far better then he, someone who could perhaps bring back the Shiny Brook of 1964 as if it were yesterday. A hypnotist.

The idea grew on the detective. What was there to lose? And Myra was willing. Yes, she'd allow herself to be put into a trance, go back to being 22 again when she had driven a white Mini van up there.

Topping had taken a hypnotist to the Moor to allow him

177

to see the landscape for himself so that he would know exactly what Myra was talking about. Everyone agreed it would be an exercise well worth undertaking: Topping, his men, Myra, her solicitor, certainly Winnie Johnson. Everyone, that is, except the Home Secretary. No, said Douglas Hurd after considering the request that Myra Hindley had made herself. He was not sufficiently persuaded about the value of information obtained under hypnosis.

Winnie Johnson was upset by the decision. She wrote to the Home Office, but officials refused to be moved. It would serve no useful purpose. Mrs Johnson got a nice, thoughtfully-worded letter, but in the end it amounted to the same. Sorry. The tears stained her face once again. As she had once said to me, and they were words she often repeated: "There is nothing worse, no fate more terrible, than not knowing. I just want Keith found, wherever he is, so that he can be buried properly, so that I know where he is and I can put some flowers on his grave...every day I pray that my agony will end."

Saddleworth Moor was now deserted, cloaked by winter, silent, still concealing one of the loneliest graves in the world beneath the now hard peat.

Two hundred miles away, a decision had been made in London. The files on the case, sent to him by Peter Topping, had been carefully, studied by the Director of Public Prosecutions, Allan Green. And on Thursday, 14 January 1988 he announced the verdict.

It was a ruling that caused Ann West to declare her disgust and Paul Reade to seek legal advice.

The families were told it would "not be in the public interest" for Ian Brady and Myra Hindley to stand trial again.

WITH a quiet dignity that hid their grief and wearing their best suits, Amos Reade and his son Paul sat down in the light oak-panelled courtroom, now filling up with reporters, and waited silently for the start of what they knew would be a great ordeal: the inquest on Pauline. They would finally learn the cause of her death and a verdict would be delivered by the jury of five men and three women now shuffling into their seats.

Every chair in the room at Oldham magistrates' court was occupied as coroner Bryan North took his seat and faced the jurors. It would be rather surprising, he told them, if they had no prior knowledge of events that had occurred on Saddleworth Moor some twenty-odd years ago, but he wanted them to disregard anything they had heard, read or seen and concentrate on the evidence that would be put before them that morning. The sole purpose of this hearing was to find the cause of death of Pauline Reade, not to decide any culpability or criminality. That was for another place. Paul Reade glanced at the man sitting next to him, Peter Birkett, the barrister he hoped would be representing their family in *another place*. He wanted his sister's murderers to stand trial.

He looked again at the coroner, still talking to the jury..."who left her home, 9 Wiles Street, Gorton, on 12 July 1963 to attend a dance at a local club, but never arrived and has never been seen alive since..."

Mr North looked at his jurors. "You will have to view certain photographs that show the area and the location in which the body was found. There is no doubt you will find these unpleasant and if anyone appears to become unwell I will adjourn if necessary to allow them to compose themselves." The five men and three women, some of whom would now have been younger, had she lived, than the 16-year-old girl they were about to see, in death, fidgeted.

Detective Chief Superintendent Peter David Topping, now dark-suited, white handkerchief in his breast pocket (most of the reporters had previously only seen him in an anorak or boiler suit), took the witness stand to tell of the new wave of public interest in 1985 and 1986 that had caused him to reopen the files on the missing children and decide to review the case thoroughly, and of how it had all led to the discovery of Pauline on Hollin Brow Knoll.

Slowly, calmly, hiding any feelings one father might have for another, seated only a few feet away, he described the position of her body, the state of her clothing. *The dress and underskirt pulled up above the waist. No knickers*. It was a familiar hallmark, one I recognised from the evidence at the trial for three other murders of Brady and Hindley. I was sitting among the reporters, behind the father, the brother. I knew their knuckles would be white.

I recalled the words of the prosecuting Attorney-General at Chester Castle in May 1966 as he spoke of the three murders: "*There was present not only a sexual element, but an abnormal sexual element, a perverted sexual element*."

Edward Evans..."*evidence that the youth's trousers had been down*." Lesley Ann Downey...*photographed "naked in various pornographic positions*." John Kilbride... "*trousers pulled down to mid-thigh, underpants rolled in a band and knotted at the back*."

The photographs of Pauline, neatly arranged in folders, were handed to the jury, to be examined, page by page, with commentary by Peter Topping. One: Excavations and a white shoe. Two: Careful excavations around the find. Three: A foot in a white shoe. Four: This shows the body we recovered from Saddleworth Moor. That page was turned very slowly. Five: The injury to the neck of the victim. The five men and three women would never forget it. Amos Reade was asked if he wanted to see the photographs. He shook his head. No, thank you.

"In the course of my inquiries," said Peter Topping, "I found it necessary to interview Myra Hindley and Ian Brady on a number of occasions. On the conclusion of my enquiries I submitted a report of the file to the office of the Director of Public Prosecutions for his consideration. In January 1988 he announced he was of the opinion that it was not in the public interest for criminal proceedings to be taken in respect of the death of Pauline Reade." Enquiries into her death were closed as far as he was concerned.

The barrister, Peter Birkett, rose. "Would you be in a

position, from the knowledge you have obtained, to describe the *precise* circumstances in which she came to meet her death?''

It was a question that had nagged Paul Reade, tortured him since he first realised that his sister had not just been another missing person, that she had met her murderers in the back streets of Gorton. However, it was not a question which could be given an elaborate answer in this court. The question was rephrased. *Did* he have *that* information? "I have received information which, if it is correct, could lead me to answer that I *do* have that sort of information," replied Topping, slowly, quietly, carefully.

Amos and Paul Reade listened as Dr Geoffrey Garrett described the examination that had been made on Pauline. The remarkable preservation of her body that, though it had been impossible to tell if she had been sexually assaulted, had revealed its dreadful injuries. That to her head, and the horrible – unbelievable that one human could do that to another – wound to her throat, so brutal it had cut through her spine. They bowed their heads, as they had at her funeral. Thank God Joan wasn't here to hear all this and had stayed at home, to put some flowers on Pauline's grave and remember her how she was. No, Mr Reade had no questions to ask the doctor.

Mr North turned to the jury. Pauline, he told them, had somehow been lured to that isolated spot and it was more than likely that it was there that she met her death. "You may find these proceedings puzzling in that names have been named and allegations made in relation to certain persons for complicity in the death of Pauline. But there is a clear rule which precludes you from bringing in any verdict which in any way names any person as being responsible." The only verdict open to them, in his opinion, was that Pauline had been killed unlawfully.

The eight people took only five minutes to agree unanimously with the coroner. The proceedings had taken an hour, but before the court was cleared Mr North called Peter Topping back to the stand. "I am well aware that at times you have conducted your enquiries in the face of considerable scepticism and ill-judged comment," he said. He was aware that Topping and his team had battled in a harsh terrain and in harsh weather, and felt it was their dogged determination that had successfully concluded the case and brought comfort to Pauline's family. "You have upheld and enhanced the reputation of the police force," he told the detective. Twin spots of colour touched Topping's cheeks. He nodded. "Thank you, sir."

The coroner's remarks were to be endorsed by the man who had been Topping's fiercest critic, MP Geoffrey Dickens, who was gracious enough to admit later that – although in some instances he had been only echoing public opinion in the area – he had been somewhat hasty in his remarks.

Did he now feel vindicated? someone asked Topping afterwards. "That is not a word I would have used," he said. "The enquiry was always justified." And Keith Bennett? "The case remains open. However, I have no further information on which I could launch any new search. We have reached the point now where we have no information on which we can justifiably act." Yes, he had submitted a request for Myra Hindley to be subjected to hypnosis to the Home Secretary, but he had decided he would not allow it. Topping shrugged. "That, in many ways, has closed the door on my taking the search any further."

The CID chief was still convinced that hypnosis might unlock the final secret from the mind of the murderess and he found it difficult to hide his frustration. "You know", he said, "it was just a small piece of seemingly insignificant information that led me to find the grave of Pauline Reade.

The clue needed to find Keith could have been provided by hypnotism. "It has been used in the past to uncover information in criminal cases," he said. "I feel there is everything to gain and nothing to lose by it. I would like the Home Secretary to reconsider in this case, for the sake of Mrs Johnson."

Winnie Johnson, meanwhile, was saying: "I'm the only

victim's parent whose child has not been found and properly buried. It seems I'll never put flowers on Keith's grave." It was natural that she should have felt, in her torment and frustration, that perhaps the police were not doing enough. Had they *really* followed up every clue, searched everywhere they could? The determined mother reached a decision.

She would go to Saddleworth Moor herself.

★   ★   ★

MRS Johnson stepped from the police Land Rover, shielded her eyes against the spring sunshine, and looked around her. So this was it, the place where her little lad had been brought, nearly 24 years ago.

In warm slacks and anorak she was a small figure against the backcloth of rocks, ravines and gullies that surrounded her. The man by her side, Peter Topping, spoke kindly, gently. They'd walk along the rough-surfaced water board track, to the area where he and his men had been searching. She looked around her again. Never, even in her many tormented dreams, had she been in an area so totally desolate, so vast.

She had gone to the Moor because she had to see for herself, satisfy herself that no stone had been left unturned, no suspicion ignored and, perhaps, to seek comfort in being as close as she could possibly get to her long-lost son. Peter Topping had agreed to her request to be shown the area where he and his team had finally run out of clues and reluctantly called off the search.

He took her there on the day after the inquest on Pauline Reade, a warm, soft day that mercifully took much of the grim harshness from the landscape. Shiny Brook was a name she thought of every day. And now she was here. It was a cheerful-sounding name, not like those given to some of its brooding neighbours like the foreboding Black Hill or Black Moss. But, nonetheless, a name to chill and sadden because of its dreadful significance.

Mrs Johnson had been so distressed at the failure of the

police to find Keith that she had even said she would be prepared to dig on the Moor herself. Now, as she walked the mile to Shiny Brook, she was seeing for herself what they were up against. Her son Alan, now 34 – he would have been only ten when his older brother disappeared – was with her.

As the valley opened out, they were dwarfed by miles of moorland. She looked at Topping, who had endured all weathers in this place to try to bring her peace of mind, and was patiently pointing out the pattern of his search, and knew that no man could have done more. She walked, past the glistening reservoir, in the footsteps of Ian Brady and Myra Hindley, wondering if Keith had trodden that very ground and knowing he was so near, yet so far away. She blinked back the tears that were misting her spectacles. It was so silent, so still, they could hear themselves breathing. Just how far away was Keith? *Where was he*? Perhaps she would never know.

"I know now the police have done all they can," she said. "Because they hadn't found Keith's body I had thought they could have done more. But now I've seen this..." She glanced around her, her head turning slowly, her eyes taking in every feature..."Now I've seen this vast landscape and had everything explained to me I know they've done a magnificent job."

The policemen gently helped Mrs Johnson back into the Land Rover. Coming here was something she had felt she ought to do, said Topping. "We are trying to fulfil that wish in the kindest way we can. What she wants most of all is to find her son's body." But, he said softly: "I can't give her any hope." He shrugged helplessly. "There is no hope to give."

Winnie Johnson left the Moor. Both she and Topping knew there was only one person in this world who could help now. She would "fight and fight and then fight some more" to get that help, to get the Home Secretary to change his mind about allowing *her* to be hypnotised. "As long as I draw breath I'll never give up," she vowed. The mind of the 22-year-old Myra Hindley must be freed to return to Saddleworth Moor. She *must* remember. A tear stole down Mrs Johnson's cheek.

Until then, there could be no flowers for Keith.

ON Friday, 15 April 1988 Paul Reade was back at the magistrates court at Oldham where, three days earlier, he had heard of the terrible way in which his sister had died. This time he was there to try to put Ian Brady and Myra Hindley back in the dock for murder. He successfully applied, with his lawyers, for a summons to be issued to take out a private prosecution. His satisfaction, though, was short-lived. Within a matter of hours the Director of Public Prosecutions brought a halt to the criminal proceedings. Paul Reade said he would fight on.

He would never forget the night of 12 July 1963. Or forgive.

CONCLUSION

NUMBER 16 Wardle Brook Avenue, Hattersley is no more. On an autumn day in 1987, very much like the day on which the door was opened to a policeman's knock to reveal to the world the horror the house had hidden, the workmen came. Brick by brick they dismantled the end house of the terrace of four, a house that had frightened its tenants and now had drawn the sightseers. The house where Ian Brady and Myra Hindley had, as people used to say in 1965, lived in sin. A shocking, almost unbelievable sin.

The workmen took away the bricks, the mortar, the wood, the glass. Today, the gable rebuilt, with Number 14 now the end house, it is as if Number 16 had never existed, wiped from the face of the earth. Out of sight, but never out of mind. There are those it will haunt forever. For the deeds of Ian Brady and Myra Hindley outlast bricks and mortar. They cannot be dismantled as if they had never existed.

On 12 July 1963 and again on 16 June 1964, the perfect crime, the perfect murder, was committed. In the second case so perfect that to this day not even the perpetrators can find the evidence, the poor little body of Keith Bennett, so carefully concealed all those years ago. The murderers have both been back to Saddleworth Moor twice, returned to the scene of their crimes. For don't they say the murderer, the perfect murderer, always returns to the scene of his crime?

Isn't falling to the temptation of having to boast to someone always their undoing? Just as, in 1965, Ian Brady had to brag to David Smith that he had committed the perfect murders (*"I've killed three or four..."*)

Brady, 20 years after his trial, had started to boast again, begun to talk, broken the silence that he and Myra had kept for so long, the secrets that still bound them together. (*"If I revealed what really happened Myra would not get out in 100 years."*) The murderer was returning in his mind, dangerously in his words, to the scene of his crimes, *their* crimes. Was it the prelude to a final gesture, a full confession, before his death? At the time he was greatly emaciated and there were rumours that he was terminally ill, and he had spoken of suicide.

Myra Hindley had had an obsessive, insatiable hunger for freedom and could see her final, slender hopes were under threat. If Ian Brady talked, confessed, before she did and the long-buried bodies of children were found then her silence would damn her. Imprison her forever, body and soul.

On a November day in 1986, slowly, cautiously at first, she began to lay her cards on the table, staking all on a gamble that she would win public support and sympathy. She showed more and more of her hand until there was no turning back, even risking being returned to the dock and setting in motion an astonishing chain of events that even brought cooperation with the authorities from Ian Brady.

She says she has changed. Certainly there has been an amazing change in her attitude to her crimes. And in that of Ian Brady. But, it seems, they will find little mercy from those who have judged them in *this* world. They are still *Evil Myra, Evil Brady*.

A quarter of a century ago, when they were young, they followed the devil on a journey to hell. It was on a one-way ticket.

The Devil's Disciples, I believe, have no more fears for the judges, the juries, the docks, the courts, the prisons, the punishments of Earth. She is now in her forty-seventh year, he in his fifty-first. Two-thirds of their three score years and ten have gone. Oh yes, they feel remorse, certainly regrets. Myra Hindley obviously clings to the belief that confession is good for the soul. Ian Brady, Godless in his youth, is likely to be hedging his bets.

For one day, the only escape from the hell they created

for themselves in the backstreets of Gorton, on Saddleworth Moor and at Number 16 Wardle Brook Avenue, will perhaps be to throw themselves on the dreadful Day of Judgement, on the mercy of *the* Supreme Court, on that of Him who said:

"Woe be unto you that cause one of these, my little ones, to stumble. It were better for that person that a millstone were hung around his neck and thrown in the depths of the sea."

As the minister, facing that hushed, shocked congregation at the funeral of little Lesley Ann Downey on 26 October 1965, had said: "The justice, wrath, and punishment of God will, I fear, be terrible – terrible indeed. It is not only a terrible crime, but an awful sin.

"And the person or persons responsible *will one day have to face God.*"

Her house is the way to hell, going down to the chambers of death.

PROVERBS, 7:27.

POSTSCRIPT: On 29 June 1988, almost exactly one year after the body of Pauline Reade was discovered, Detective Chief Superintendent Peter Topping, an old back injury aggravated by the rigours of the moors search, announced his early retirement from the Force.

Keith Bennett is still missing.